# THE VERDICT OF BIMBILLA CHIEFTAINCY

# RIGHT OR WRONG

## New Edition

**Fusheini Yakubu**

WORKBOOK PRESS LLC
187 E Warm Springs Rd,
Suite B285, Las Vegas, NV 89119, USA

| | |
|---|---|
| Website: | https://workbookpress.com/ |
| Hotline: | 1-888-818-4856 |
| Email: | admin@workbookpress.com |

Ordering Information:
Quantity sales. Special discounts are available on quantity purchases by corporations, associations, and others. For details, contact the publisher at the address above.

Library of Congress Control Number:
ISBN-13:            978-1-957618-58-6 (Paperback Version)
                    978-1-957618-59-3 (Digital Version)

REV. DATE: 02/04/2022

# THE VERDICT OF BIMBILLA CHIETAINCY RIGHT OR WRONG?

### REVISED EDITION

### BY: FUSHEINI YAKUBU

# CONTENTS

**Chapter**                                        **Page**

## PROLOGUE

Let the art speak!

Let the word speak!

Speak out to the world!

Here is what I have.

Love it or hate it.

# ACKNOWLEDGEMENT

"When you see a pregnant Nanny-Goat in the market for sale, it means there is a complicated problem in the house". This is a wise saying that reveals the reason for writing this book. Some people may be endowed with some special talents, which may be hidden. When such people are touched by some events to use the talents, the impact almost becomes beneficial to others. It is in this light I found myself.

I was touched by the judgments passed by the Judicial Committee of the Northern Region House of Chiefs, Tamale on March 13, 2012 and the Judicial Committee of the National House of Chiefs, Kumasi on Wednesday, 8th October 2014 on the Bimbilla chieftaincy case that has lasted for about 10 years.

My initial source was oral literature where I had to go from one person to another gathering data/information in relation to the issue at stake. Those who helped me in this were the following people: the late Alhaji Abdulai "Bimbilla Lung-Naa", (a local historian), Alhaji Braimah Damba (Bimbilla Tolon-Naa), Bagli Naa Yakubu Wumbei, Mr. Inusah K. Dasoli, Vo-naa Attah Abarika, Juo Regent (Osman Mahama), Mr Abu hassan (Bolahi-Naa) and Warikpamo-Naa Yahaya Abdulai.

Other sources from which I gathered my information were:

The Judicial Committee of the Nanumba Traditional Council Judgment on Bimbilla Chieftaincy case, 8th August 2003 (Gumah Commission)

The Judicial Committee of the Northern Region House of Chiefs Judgment on Bimbilla Chieftaincy case, 13th March 2012

The Judicial Committee of the National House of Chiefs Judgment on Bimbilla Chieftaincy Apeal, 8th October 2014

Ibrahim Mahama    - History and Tradition of Dagbon, 2003

Fusheini Yakubu    - History of the Gbewaa Kingdoms, Part I – New Edition, 2013

Nanumba District Profile, 1996

Nanumba District Economic Development Plan, 1996

Chieftaincy Matters -- Areas of Research, Northern Region

Peter Skalnik, Pluralism of Political Culture in Nanung, 1992

Judgment of the Supreme Court of Ghana 2018 on Bimbilla Chieftaincy Dispute

Many people have contributed to the production of the book whose names did not appear. To them I say: Thank you.

Finally, I thank God (Almighty Allah) for the good health, time, and other resources he has granted me to produce this book.

Thank you.

Fusheini Yakubu

# INTRODUCTION

"When you see a Toad running in a broad daylight it means something is chasing it". This is a wise saying that is true with this book because, it is a presentation on the rotational gate system of Nanung and analysis of the judgment passed by the Judicial Committee of the Northern Region House of Chiefs, Tamale on 13<sup>th</sup> March 2012, the Judicial Committee of the National House Chiefs, Kumasi on 8<sup>th</sup> October 2014 with suit number: NHC. INR/2012 and the Supreme Court of Ghana in 2018.

The main aim of the writer is to educate readers on the fundamentals of the rotational gate system of Nanung as well as its tradition and custom.

The second problem the book seeks to solve is to conserve and protect the tradition and custom of Nanung. Nanung kingdom was one of the German colonies in the 18<sup>th</sup> century. Due to the short stay of the Germans because of the first and second world wars, Nanung has not received the needed documentation. The only documentation on Nanung is oral literature; as such, it is prone to distortions by individuals to suit their interest as it is being passed on from generation to generation.

The presentation contained in this book is an objective analysis of the judgment passed by both the Judicial Committees of the Northern Region and National House of Chiefs and the Supreme Court of Ghana in the interest of Nanung tradition and custom. It is not to favour any of the two-chieftaincy factions. However, if two people are fighting over something, definitely there is a righteous one among them. Again, this is not to say the analysis, or the writer is biased. The custom and tradition of Nanung is of paramount interest to the writer. It is also to challenge the justice system of Ghana in relation to the verdict: a case study of Bimbilla Chieftaincy Verdict by the Northern Region House of Chiefs, National House Chiefs, and the Supreme Court of Ghana. As human institution, certain external or internal pressures be it political, social, religious, economical, influence of some Kingdom institutions, bodies or individual characters do compromise justice for jury.

Initially, I titled this book *"The Rotational Gate System of Nanung"*. Many students from various tertiary institutions have referenced and cited this title in their respective project assignments. However, the judgment of the National House Chiefs on 8th October 2014 prompted me to update the book before publication. As part of the review process there was the need for more specific and focus title for the book. Hence; ***"The Verdict of Bimbilla Chieftaincy: Right or Wrong?"*** Students who have used either of these titles are still valid.

# DEDICATION

I am dedicating this book to my late grandfather, Alhaji Abdulai (Bimbilla Lung-Naa) who showered on me the oral literature during his lifetime. *Granddad, it is through your effort that I have been able to produce this book. You are gone for good but left us a legacy. There is nothing on earth that may be beneficial to you at this moment apart from prayers. May your soul rest in perfect peace.* Amen.

# CHAPTER 1

## 1.0 NANUNG KINGDOM.

Nanung Kingdom is one of the three main Gbewaa Kingdoms in Northern Ghana. The Gbewaa Kingdoms comprise Dagbon, Mamprugu and Nanung. These Kingdoms were founded by the three great sons of Naa Gbewaa namely: Tohagu, Gmantambu, and Nyagsi, son of Sitobu. According to Shinnie and Ozanne, the archaeological evidence conducted at Yani Dabari (old Yendi), Naa Gbewaa came to Great Dagbon (Modern Dagbon, Mamprugu and Nanung) in the 13 centuries. These Gbewaa sons broke away at Bagli/Namburugu in the 14[th]century and founded their individual Kingdoms. Naa Gmantambu went towards the east and founded the Nanung Kingdom with the Nanumbas. (*For more information on Nanung Kingdom, refer to the History of the Gbewaa Kingdoms chapter 4 by Fusheinu Yakubu, 2013*).

According to the Nanumba District profile, Nanung Kingdom is located between Latitude 8.5° N & 9.25° N and Longitude 0.5°E & 0.5°W of the Greenwich Meridian, which more or less divides the traditional area into two parts. The Nanung Kingdom is found in the eastern corridor of the Northern Region of Ghana and shares boundary with:

-Yendi Municipal to the north.

-Zabzugu and Tatale Districts and the Republic of

Togo to the east.

-East Gonja to the west and southwest; and

-Nkwanta South District of the Volta Region to the southeast

Nanung occupies a total land area of about 4520 square km and has three administrative districts namely, Nanumba-North Municipal, Nanumba-South District and Nkwanta-North District *(Nanumba District Profile, 1996)*.

## 1.1 Climate and Rainfall.

Nanung lies in the Tropical continental climatic zone with the mid-day sun always overhead. As a result, day temperatures are fairly high ranging between 29 degrees Celsius and 41 degrees Celsius and occasionally reading 45 degrees Celsius. Like any other part of the West African sub-region, Nanung comes under the influence of the wet southwest monsoon and dry northeast trade winds. The area experiences a single maximum rainfall regime with annual rainfall averaging 1363 mm with most of it falling within six months (May – October) leaving the other half of the year dry i.e., when the region comes under the dry North East Trade winds. During this period evaporation and transpiration is very high, grass dries out, and bush fires becomes rampant creating an acute water shortage *(Nanumba District Profile, 1996)*.

According to the Nanumba District Profile, maximum rainfall is recorded in September. During this period, streams and rivers overflow their banks and there is a lot of surface run-off. The result of this type of rainfall pattern is that there is a single cropping season.

## 1.2 Drainage and Vegetation.

Streams and rivers as well as man-made dams and dugouts drain the traditional area. The two main rivers include the Daka, which spans 145km of the western border of the traditional area with East Gonja and the Oti River, which meanders north south across the eastern part with a total of 85 km within the traditional area. Others include Kumar and Kumbo rivers and their tributaries, which occasionally break into series of pools during the long dry season. There are dams created in Bimbilla, Wulensi, Lungni, Bakpaba, Dakpam, Binda, Nassamba, Nakpaa-Gbeini, Gambuga, Juo, Kpassa and so on. According to Nanumba District Economic Development Plan, there is also a gorge found near Juale, which has been designated as a hydroelectric site on River Oti.

De-vegetation of the banks and catchments areas of these streams/rivers resulting from farming and the annual bush fires has led to the siltation and drying up of some of these water bodies *(Nanumba District Economic Development Plan, 1996).*

The district has an encouraging ground water potential as well. By a GAP (Ghana Water and Sewerage Assistant Project) study 1996, titled "Population and Water demand data for the three Northern Regions", ground water resources for the area are 55% and 22% for hand pump and mechanization, respectively.

The vegetation type found in the area is the Guinea-Savannah with tall grass (particularly elephant grass) interspersed with drought and fire-resistant trees. Some of the tree species are the Shea-nut, Dawadawa, and few Baobab trees *(Nanumba District Economic Development Plan, 1996).*

## 1.3 Soil characteristics.

Soils are characteristically heavy and dark coloured. By Soil Research Institute and Council for Scientific and Industrial Research (SRI/CSIR) classifications, types of soils found in the area are the savannah ochrosols, savannah glysols and ground water laterite.

## 1.4 Ethnicity.

The indigenous ethnic group in the area is the Nanumbas. Other ethnic groups include Kotokolis, Bassaries, Nawuris, Ewes, some Akans, Anuffor and Konkombas. The traditional area has about 450 communities occupied by the above-mentioned ethnic groups *(Nanumba District Profile, 1996)*.

## 1.5 Agriculture.

The major occupation of the people is agriculture. Conservative indications are that about 85% of the people are in this sector. Crops grown are roots and tubers, cereals, legumes, and tree crops such as cashew and teak. The district is a net exporter of legumes and roots & tubers. Farmers in yam cultivation mostly employ the bush fallow method in particular and Konkombas mostly practice shifting cultivation. Moreover, this has some effects on the provision of boreholes and toilet facilities *(Nanumba District Profile, 1996)*.

## 1.6 Tourism and Investment Potentials.

According to the Nanumba District Economic Development Plan, the tourism sector remains unexploited and tourism infrastructure is undeveloped.

However, the district has a few guesthouses operated by some individuals and institutions and these include GNAT, Nanumba North District Assembly, Junior Original, Work & Happiness, Aziz Guest House, Natogmah Guest House located in Wulensi and Catholic guest houses which are woefully inadequate.

### 1.6.1 Tourism Potentials.

Tourism potentials that exist in the district include among others:

- Kukuo scarp (*where elderly women between the ages of 60 – 80 years descend to futch water and climb*)
- Kuku Witches shrine (*where alleged witches are administered with concoction to neutralize their spiritual powers.*)
- Kpalga Ancient Mosque (*Slave Mosque where Arab Slave Raiders observed prayers during the trans-sahara trade.*)
- Chichagi Ancient Mosque (*Slave Mosque where Arab Slave Raiders observed prayers during the trans-sahara trade.*)
- *Chebto* Ancient Pots and Shrine at Kpatinga village (*mystery ancient pots.*)
- *Pinaa* Cave and Shrine at Kpatingavillage (*Thomb of a great warrior, Bakpaba Naa Iddrisah*)
- Fetish Groves:

- *Bokpinga* in Bimbilla, noted for black scorpions and for the attraction of rain.

- Nakpaa-Gbeini Grove has a special water body from which the Nakpaa-naa is prohibited from drinking or eating a fish from it.

- Dakpam grove noted for its wild crocodiles and is significant as far as the Bangyili gate of Nanumba Kingdom is concerned.
- Dalaayili Grove, where the **Damli** (the Staff by any enskinned Bimbilla-naa is).
- Juole Defense-Wall.
- Gorge on the Oti River.
- Colonial bunker at Wulensi.

- Chieftaincy and traditional festivals.

## 1.6.2 Major Attractions of the Nanung Kingdom

**The location of the Kingdom**: The position of the Kingdom offers itself as a gateway to the Northern sector of the country along the eastern corridor as well as the shortest route from neighbouring Burkina Faso, Benin to the south of Ghana and from south of the country to anywhere in the north enrooted to those countries.

Secondly, there are vast tract of fertile arable land suitable for commercial agriculture as well as for other economic ventures. Almost all of its irrigation potential runs into thousands of hectors and remain untapped. Labour force is available and could readily support any investment.

# NANUNG STATE

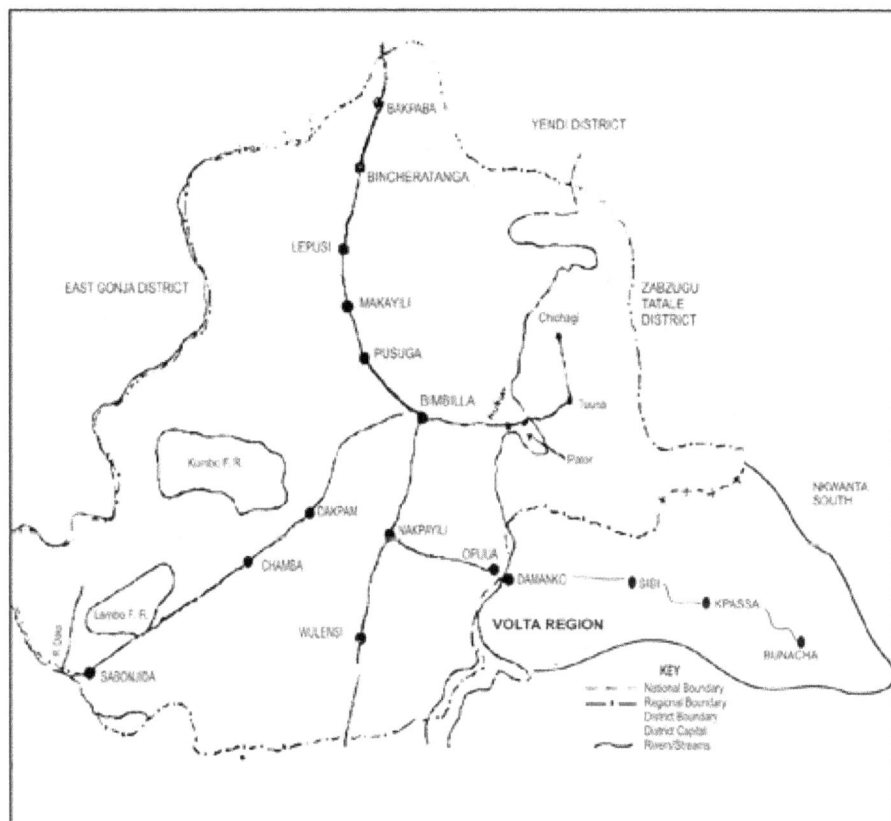

# CHAPTER 2

## NANNUNG CHIEFDOM

## 2.0 Origin of Nanung Chiefdom

According to oral literature, the Bimbilla skin title "Nam" and for that matter Nanung kingdom, was founded by Naa Gmantambu in the late 14[th]century. Naa Gmantambu is one of the three great sons of Naa Gbewaa (Naa Sitobu, Naa Tohagu & Gmantambu). According to Shinnie and Ozanne, 1972 excavations at Yani Dabari proved that Naa Gbewaa arrived in Great Dagbon (Modern Dagbon, Mamprugu & Nanung) in the 13th century. He was the one who introduced the chiefdom to the aboriginal Dagbamba and a central coordinated form of local governance system in the late 14th century. He did not achieve it on a silver platter. He fought and conquered the Tindamba (landowners or priests) who were the heads of the aboriginal Dagbamba communities. The aboriginal Dagbamba had some form of governance but the system was not centrally coordinated *(Fusheini Yakubu, History of the Gbewaa Kingdoms Part I – New Edition, 2013)*. There are no records as to when the aboriginal Dagbamba arrived in the country called Great Dagbon. One can only say they arrived in Great Dagbon several years before the advent of the rulers (Naa Gbewaa & his descendants).

According to oral literature, after the death of Naa Gbewaa, Naa Sitobu was the next chief and he was the fourth child of Naa Gbewaa. Kachiogu or Yentuare was the first daughter (*first child*) of Naa Gbewaa and according to the tradition or custom, a female child cannot inherit or aspire to the apex skin title (Nam). As such, Zirili and Kufogu fought each other over the title. Ziril killed Kufogu and died shortly and that gave Sitobu the opportunity to succeed the title after Naa Gbewaa. After some years, Naa Sitobu initiated his first son, Nyagsi one night at Bagli and mysteriously entered the ground. This led to the division of the Gbewaa Kingdom into three sister Kingdoms: Modern Dagbon, Mamprugu & Nanung. The table below is an illustration of the three main Gbewaa Kingdoms:

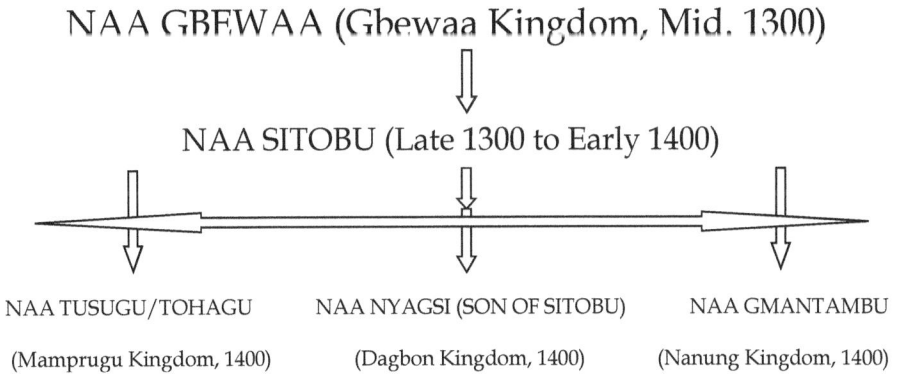

NAA GBEWAA (Gbewaa Kingdom, Mid. 1300)
⇓
NAA SITOBU (Late 1300 to Early 1400)

| NAA TUSUGU/TOHAGU | NAA NYAGSI (SON OF SITOBU) | NAA GMANTAMBU |
|---|---|---|
| (Mamprugu Kingdom, 1400) | (Dagbon Kingdom, 1400) | (Nanung Kingdom, 1400) |

According to some writers, that Naa Gmantambu did not desert Naa Sitobu or his son Naa Nyagsi. It was rather Naa Nyagsi who pointed out: "*Doli Naa Nuu Zuʏu*", literary meaning: *Follow this direction of the Chief,* pointing to a particular direction to Naa Gmantambu the area he should establish his own Kingdom. In addition, that marked the beginning of the name Nanumba. This is more of a rumour than an oral tradition source.

The ethnic name "Nanumba" is a corrupted Nawuri statement whenever Naa Gmantambu invites the Nawuris to a meeting in Bimbilla. They do make this statement in the ancient times: *"Naa Nuba"* meaning: "Go and listen and come". In those days, only few of the Nawuris could speak Dagbani/Nanunli, so those who understand the language were always chosen to attend meetings of Naa Gmantambu after which they will go back home and pass the information to others. The long stay of the Nanumbas and Nawuris, as well as inter-marriages corrupted the original Dagbani that was spoken by the aboriginal Dagbambas to the present day Nanunli dialect *(Fusheini Yakubu, History of the Gbewaa Kingdoms Part I – New Edition, 2013).*

After the confusion at Bagli, Naa Gmantambu headed towards Yeji through Salaga to Attebubu. As at then Salaga and Yeji were not in existence. The only settlement was Attebubu with temporal structures such as thatch. From Attebubu, he went towards the east and settled at Nkonya-Bunbulla in the Oti Region. From Nkonya- Bunbulla, he came up North and finally settled at Shirikpamo, now called Bimbilla. Gmantambu first settled at Daalanyili. Daalana tried rejecting him but he resisted. Kpandigli (male & female), Daalana, and Shirikpamo Tindamba attempted fighting Gmantambu.

During the fight, all the young men fled and left the chief priests. They fled to seek refuge at a village called Juo. Juo *Nabang Tindana, the chief priest of the village,* finally advised his colleagues that they cannot fight their own brother and for that matter, they accepted Gmantambu by symbols of leaves signifying peace. *'We have accepted you and you must accept us too'.* Said by Juo Nabang Tindana. Juo Nabang Tindana told Gmantambu: *my fellowships are Wumpigu Tindana as Tagnamo Naa, Gambugu Tindana, Lanjiri Tindana and Jilo Varili Tindana.* Lanjiri initial settlement was at Nahabil Zoli (Lanjiri Tuyani) before and during the time of Naa Gmantambu after which the community finally settled at the current Kukuo. Later in the night, Naa Gmantambu and Juo Nabang Tindana met and shared among themselves best cultural and traditional practices. This led to the final standardization of Bimbilla Chief's regalia/insignia by Naa Gmantambu and Juo Nabang Tindana currently referred to as Juo Naa. It is for this reason that Juo Naa became the head and only person to enskin or appoints the Bimbilla Naa. He keeps the regalia/insignia and the regalia originated from Naa Gmantambu through the Gbewa skin to Juo Nabang Tindana now the Juo Naa. *(Oral Literature of Late Bimbilla Lung-Naa Alhaji Abdulai, 2008).*

According to the late Bimbilla Lung-Naa, Naa Gmantambu mandated Juo Naa to henceforth, **to traditionally catch and perform the enskinment rites of every Bimbilla Naa (The Overload of Nanung).** Similarly, only Bimbilla Naa can appoint and perform the enskinment rites of Juo Naa.

This formed the structure of the Nanumba Traditional Council with Bimbilla Naa being the president and Juo Naa Vice President. Immediately Bimbilla Naa is pronounced dead, Juo Naa becomes the head of Nanung Kingdom. After the funeral of Bimbilla Naa is performed, Juo Naa traditional catches the next Bimbilla Naa based on the two-gate rotational system. Initially, Juo Naa does all the enskinment rites, but as the chiefdom grows, Juo Naa in consultation with Bimbilla Naa and other elders of Nanung constituted the king makers (*Salaa Kpamba*). Juo Naa then delegates the function of the enskinment rites to the other members and does only the traditional catching of the Bimbilla Naa as the head of kingmakers. Any one or body who does any installation rites contrary to the above is considered null and void and will not be recognized by the custom and tradition of Nanung as Bimbilla Naa (Overload of Nanung).

## 2.1 Elders / Kingmakers of Bimbilla Skin (Salaa Kpamba)

- ✓ Juo-Naa (head of Kingmakers)
- ✓ Tagnamo-Naa
- ✓ Gambuga-Naa
- ✓ Lanjiri-Naa
- ✓ Chichagi-Naa
- ✓ Sirikpamo-Tindana
- ✓ Jilo-Naa

Wulensi Naa was recently added to the elders. Otherwise, Wulensi Naa is a title for the priest. Another important issue concerning the elders, referred to as kingmakers is the substitution of Juole for Tagnamo. The reason of this substitution came because of Tagnamo title being transferred to Dagbon. This is because, Dagbon was the paternal side of the then Tagnamo Naa Koganalogu who went back to Dagbon with the Tagnamo title. The Tagnamo Naa Koganalogu was in Tagnamo, served his maternal uncles, and became the most elderly person among them. When Tagnamo title became vacant, they agreed for him to go to his maternal home for the title. Indeed, when he went in for the title, after which he returned to Dagbon with the Tagnamo title and said: *"When you go to your maternal home and get promoted, you have to go back to your paternal home with the promotion"*. Another old school of oral literature also indicates that the Tagnamo Naa Koganalogu had a problem with Bimbilla Naa. So, whenever the Damba festival comes, he will go and celebrate in Yendi and eventually transferred the title to Dagbon. That was during the reign of Bimbilla Naa Abdulai in the 1940s *(Oral Literature of Late Bimbilla Lung-Naa Alhaji Abdulai, 2008)*.

Tagnamo title is not lost. The male children stand the chance to retrieve the title back to Nanung because Tagnamo is Nanung skin title "Nam".

Kpatihi-Naa is not a core member of the Kingmakers but a co-opted member, who performs delegators function by Gambuga-Naa and Lanjiri-Naa, by putting the insignia on the traditional catched Bimbilla Naa by Juo-Naa. The question of fact here is: who was the first Kpatihi-Naa of the Gmantambu Chiefdom and which year was it started? Dibsi-Naa is also a co-opted member *(Oral Literature of Late Bimbilla Lung-Naa Alhaji Abdulai, 2008)*.

## 2.2 Nanumba Traditional Council

The Nanumba Traditional Council is made of the following members:

Bimbilla Naa – President

Juo Naa – Vice President

Gambuga Naa

Dakpam Naa & Nakpaa Naa

Lanjiri Naa

Suburi-Naa

Jilo Naa

Chichagi Naa

Debsi Naa

Wulensi Naa

Kpihibara Naa

Worikpamo

Tolon Naa

Jua Naa

Bakpaba Naa

Chamba Naa

Gbungbalga Naa

Kpatihi-Naa as a co-opted member *(Oral Literature by Chief Worikpamo Yahaya Abdulai, 2012)*


## 2.3 Council of Elders

The Council of Elders is made up of the following members:

Kpihibara Naa

Worikpamo

Kpihiga Naa

Tamalgu

Bomaha-Naa

Yimaha-Naa

Zayuri-Naa

Bripeil-Naa

Nbamali

Kpatihi-Naa as a co-opted member

*(Oral Literature by Chief Worikpamo Yahaya Abdulai, 2012)*

## 2.4 Some of the Tindamba in Nanung

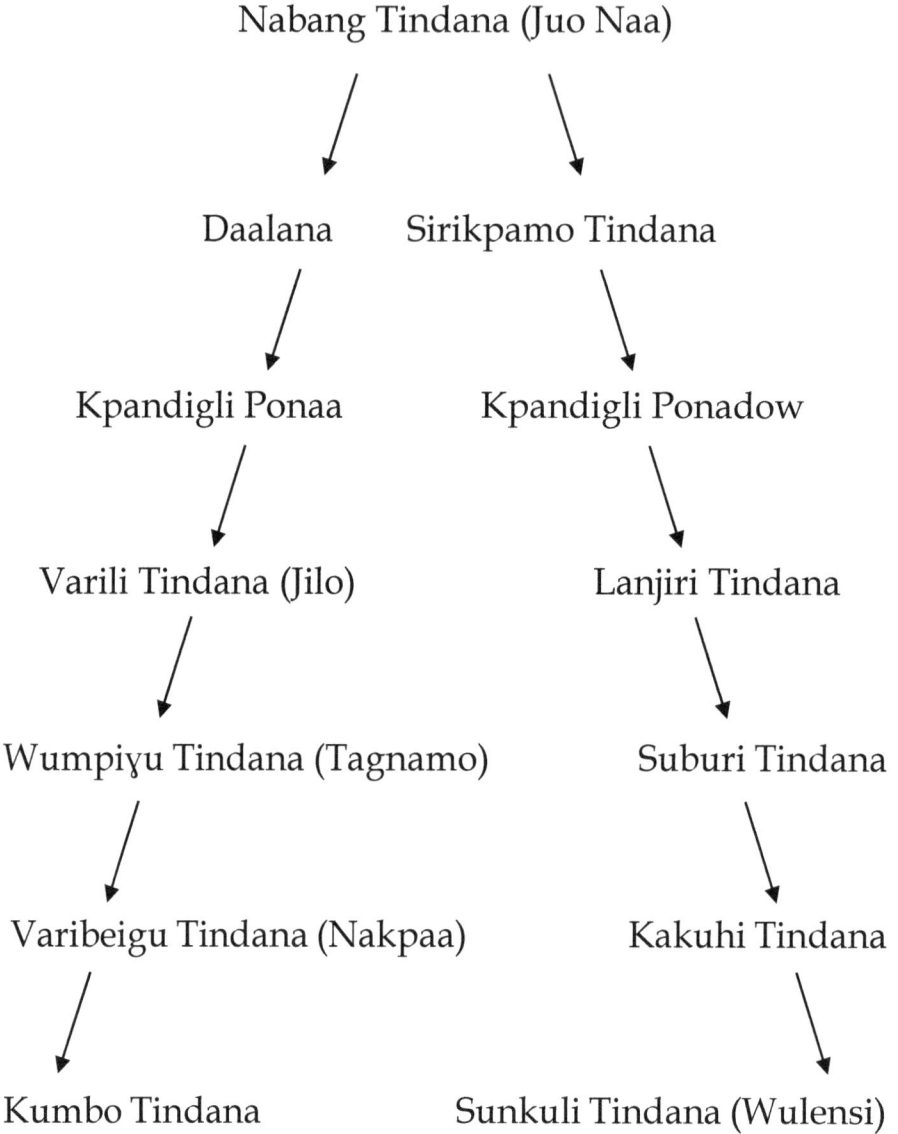

Nabang Tindana (Juo Naa)

Daalana    Sirikpamo Tindana

Kpandigli Ponaa    Kpandigli Ponadow

Varili Tindana (Jilo)    Lanjiri Tindana

Wumpiŋu Tindana (Tagnamo)    Suburi Tindana

Varibeigu Tindana (Nakpaa)    Kakuhi Tindana

Kumbo Tindana    Sunkuli Tindana (Wulensi)

*(Oral Literature of Late Bimbilla Lung-Naa Alhaji Abdulai, 2008)*

## 2.5 Functions of Kingmakers

The primary role of the Kingmakers is to enskin a Bimbilla Naa whenever the Bimbilla skin title becomes vacant. These revered chiefs play various roles in the enskinment process such as:

- Selection of the candidate: This is done by the Juo Naa as Head of the Kingmakers. He consults the Deities and gods of the Nanung land through soothsayers to reveal the most suitable candidate to him. He then informs the other Kingmakers about the revelation he has received and ask for their opinion on the candidate revealed to him and whom he has chosen. These other Kingmakers may comment on his choice but cannot enforce what they want.
- Presentation of cola nuts to the selected candidate to notify him of his elevation to the high and coveted office of Bimbilla Naa (Overload of Nanung). Juo Naa can ask any of the Kingmakers to perform this function.
- Escort of the to-be Bimbilla Naa to meet the Juo Naa at a secret location in the palace of the deceased Bimbilla Naa. This function is performed by the Langiri Naa and Gambugu Naa.
- Cleansing or bathing of the to-be Bimbilla Naa with herbal bath prepared by Juo Naa. This role is played by the Langiri Naa and Gambugu Naa under the supervision of Juo Naa.
- Standing guard at the location where these customary rites are performed on the prospective Bimbilla Naa. This is to ward off any intruders. The Guard duty is performed by the Jilo Naa, Chichagi Naa, Juali Naa and Dibsi Naa.
- Enrobement of the prospective Bimbilla Naa with the sacred regalia. This role is played by the Kpatihi Naa on the instruction of the Juo Naa.

## 2.6 Their specific roles/functions of the kingmakers are:

### 2.6.1 Juo-Naa:

Is the chairman of kingmakers of Nanung. According to the custom and tradition of Nanung, Juo Naa is responsible for the following:

- Head of kingmakers responsible for the selection of Bimbilla Naa.
- Vice president of the Nanumba Traditional Council.
- He receives Reigns of Power "Kpanjogu" from the Regent of the deceased Bimbilla Naa and his uncles, aunties, and sisters.
- Head of Tindamba in Nanung.
- Custodian of the regalia.
- He is a principal signatory at the traditional council level for the gazette of Bimbilla Naa to confirm that the enskinned Bimbilla Naa was validly selected by him as head of kingmakers.
- He is the grandfather of Nanung kingdom and gives Bimbilla Naa "Yaan-laɣfu", literary meaning token for grandchildren, during Fire Festivals.

These powers make Juo Naa the principal authority for the selection and enskinment of the Bimbilla Naa.

### 2.6.2 Gambuga-Naa:

He is next to Juo-Naa and for that matter second in command. Gambuga-Naa is responsible for the following:

- Gambuga-Naa is the custodian for the Red Fist.
- He put the Red Fist on the selected Bimbilla-Naa after the regalia during the enskinment of Bimbilla-Naa.
- He is consulted by Juo-Naa during the selection of the Bimbilla-Naa.

### 2.6.3 Lanjiri-Naa:

He is third in command and performs delegated functions during the selection and enskinment of Bimbilla-Naa. In addition, he does the following:

- He notifies the selected candidate by presenting him with cola nuts. The Kpatihi Naa accompanies him to do the presentation.
- He escorts the Bimbilla Naa selected to the old palace of the late Bimbilla-Naa for enskinment rites to be performed with the assistance of Kpatihi-Naa.
- He also escorts the newly enskinned Bimbilla-Naa back to his home for confinement and takes care of him for seven days while he is in confinement.

These three kingmakers listed above are core in the selection and enskinment process of the Bimbilla Naa. The rest of the members namely, Chichagi-Naa, Jilo-Naa, Juali-Naa, Wulehi-Naa and Debsi-Naa play consultative roles during the selection of Bimbilla-Naa. The Wulehi Naa performs post enskinment rites (He is the first to perform cultural dance at the newly enskinned Bimbilla Naa palace before another chief or group of persons can perform cultural dance at the palace). The Kpatihi Naa serves as an errand person to the other kingmakers and also stays with the newly enskinned Bimbilla Naa during his confinement as part of the enskinment process.

Juo-Naa life is at risk, for, he will mysteriously die should he dare make a mistake in selecting a wrong person as the Bimbilla Naa. It is highly believed that the selection of wrong choice to this throne is highly prohibited. This customary practice and tradition is unique to Nanung chiefdom and Nanumbas have lived with it for centuries before the advent of the German colony in the 18<sup>th</sup> century.

No international convention or constitution can alter Nanung customary practice, norms and tradition as far as standard legal practices and procedures are concerned. Only Nanumbas can employ standard legal practices and procedures to alter some of the customary practices, norms, and traditions they deem fit to do so. That is, there must be a sitting president (Bimbilla Naa) of the Nanumba Traditional Council, the vice president (Juo Naa) and the motion must be supported by two-third majority of valid members present at the meeting for consideration and approval.

## 2.7 The Gazette of Bimbilla Naa

The gazette of Bimbilla Naa begins at the Nanumba Traditional Council level. Signatories to the gazette process include:

**Juo Naa: He** is a principal signatory to the gazette, as the head of kingmakers to confirm that the newly enskinned Bimbilla Naa was validly selected by him.

**The Regent of the Late Bimbilla Naa:** is a signatory to the gazette of the newly enskinned Bimbilla Naa to confirm that he was the successor to his late father (Late Bimbilla Naa) and successfully handed over the authority (the ornamented Tiger skin, Lion skin, Leopard skin and

24

Cow skins) including the Talking Drums.

**Nakpaa Naa or Dakpam Naa** (depending on the gate to succeed): Nakpaa Naa or Dakpam Naa is also a signatory to the gazette of Bimbilla Naa as the highest title holders of the two royal gates (Bang-yili & Gbuguma-yili) to witness the gazette.

**Worikpamo and Kpihibara-Naa**: are also signatories to the gazette of Bimbilla Naa as members of council of elders and Nanumba Traditional council to witness the gazette.

**The Registrar of Nanumba Traditional Council**: is a signatory to the gazette of Bimbilla Naa as the administrator of the Nanumba Traditional Council.

After the above-mentioned signatories had endorsed the gazette document, it is then forwarded to the Regional and National Houses of Chiefs for confirmation. Final copies of the gazette document are kept at the National and Regional House Chiefs as well as the Traditional Council, respectively.

# CHAPTER 3

## THE ROTATIONAL GATES SYSTEM TITLES OF NANUNG.

### 3.0 The Evolution of the Rotational Gate System Titles.

The development and growth of Nanung chiefdom necessitated the rotational gate system initiated by Dakpam Naa Kpanjogu and Naa Gbuguma (Naa Azumah) in collaboration with Imam Mahama Walji. From the reign of Naa Gmantambu to Naa Sulgu who was the 13ᵗʰ Bimbilla chief, succession to the Bimbilla skin title "Nam" was not well defined by the custom and tradition of Nanung. As a result, succession disputes occurred repeatedly to the Bimbilla skin/title lives and properties were lost. The last succession dispute before the rotational gate system started was between Naa Damba and Naa Sulgu in the 16ᵗʰ century *(Oral Literature of Late Bimbilla Lung-Naa Alhaji Abdulai, 2008)*.

According to oral literature, Naa Sulgu came from the Suburi gate of Bimbilla and was the regent of Bimbilla Naa Wobgu {Bimbilla Naa Mahamudu). After the death of Naa Sulgu's father, Naa Saa-kpani (Naa Damba) performed the funeral of Naa Wobgu and made Naa Sulgu the regent. After the funeral, Naa Saa-kpani was enskinned the Bimbilla Naa. He gave Suburi to the regent of Naa Wobgu (Naa Sulgu). Naa Sulgu went to the old Suburi settlement. It is of late that the Suburi family moved to Bimbilla. Previously, the family was at the old Suburi settlement, located after Nanung Karaga and had its own land.

Naa Sulgu was always paying homage to his father (Naa Damba). He did it every morning and further in the afternoons. He further extended it to the evenings and in the night, for consultations. The society was convinced that, there was a good relationship between Suburi Naa (Naa Sulgu) and Naa Damba. Not knowing that, he was doing all this to examine the strength and ability of Naa Damba to fight as well as the period that Naa Damba was always alone at the palace for him to plan an attack. Indeed, Suburi Naa (Naa Sulgu) attacked Naa Damba early in the day when all the strong men from the palace had left for farm and killed him. He extended the fight to Dakpam and drove away Dakpam Naa Kpanjogu as well as Nakpaa Naa Azuma. The reason why he drove these two chiefs away was to prevent counterattack by Nakpaa Naa Azuma and Dakpam Naa Kpanjogu. Because Naa Damba and Dakpam Naa Kpanjogu were children of Naa Nyelinbolgu including Nakpaa Naa Sanboni whose mother was a different woman. Nakpaa Naa Sanboni gave birth to Nakpaa Naa Azuma (Naa Gbuguma). *(Oral Literature of Late Bimbilla Lung-Naa Alhaji Abdulai, 2008).*

Nakpaa Naa Azuma initially left for Kparigu and finally proceeded to Bassari. After some time in Bassari, he had confusion with the Bassaris, and fought with the Bassaris and conquered them. When he got to the Bimbilla Skin, he was appellated as "Bassari Dabari Zaanda" meaning the conqueror of Bassaris. According to the genealogy of Yani chiefs, Nanumbas fought Bassaris first before Naa Abdulai Nayibiegu from Dagbon. Dakpam Naa Kpanjogu also left for Chumbrum (Krachi area) and finally proceeded to the present-day Ivory Coast. All these movements were preparations to fight Naa Sulgu back. By his investigations in the Ivory Coast, they told him to return home at that time. He would be successful as at that period (during the month of Iddl-Adha by Islamic and local calendar). He came back to Dakpam and erected some thatch temporal structures and final put-up permanent structures. His followers informed Naa Sulgu that, Dakpam Naa Kpanjogu came back and settled in Dakpam again. Naa Sulgu gathered his elders, told them not to attempt him and should be allowed to stay, when Damba Festival is due, they will go and capture him live by hand. So that he would be used for sacrifice to celebrate Damba. *(Oral Literature of Late Bimbilla Lung-Naa Alhaji Abdulai, 2008)*

The man who started Chief "Imamship" was in the person of Malam Mahama Walji. He was a Hausa by tribe from Nigeria. He was a businessperson trading in cattle, donkeys, and horses. The Chichagi – Bimbilla and Bimbilla-Salaga route was an international road for the Trans-Saharan trade, with businesspersons and traders from Togo, Nigeria and other countries used to southern Ghana for trade. Malam Mahama Walji was passing through Bimbilla with his animals and Naa Sulgu intercepted the animals and killed all the first batch of animals. Malam Mahama Walji proceeded to Dakpam with his second batch of animals, where he observed prayers. After he finished the normal Salat prayers, he had begun praying to God against the Bimbilla Chief (Naa Sulgu). The community members heard him mentioning the Bimbilla chief's name and they went and informed Dakpam Naa Kpanjogu. He invited Malam Mahama Walji and asked why he mentioned Bimbilla chief's name in his prayers. He told Dakpam Naa that Naa Sulgu killed his animals and chased some away. It is for this reason that, he prayed against him. Dakpam Naa indicated to him that, Naa Sulgu fought him and Nakpaa Naa Azuma and burnt the whole community after he succeeded the late Bimbilla Naa (Naa Damba) through an attack and that he had just returned to settle in the community. He said, "*as at now I do not know where Nakpaa Naa Azuma is. I even heard, Naa Sulgu is preparing to attack me again, capture me live by hand and use me as Damba animal for the festival on the 2nd of the Month of Damba by the local calendar*". Based on the discussions between Dakpam Naa Kpanjogu and Malam Mahama Walji, an agreement was reached for Malam Mahama Walji to support Dakpam Naa Kpanjogu in his preparation for the attack by Naa Sulgu. Indeed, Naa Sulgu did attack them and with the support of Malam Mahama Walji, Dakpam Naa Kpanjogu conquered Naa Sulgu Warriors at Dakpam and proceeded with the fight to Bimbilla, where Naa Sulgu fled through the backdoor of his palace. Dakpam Naa Kpanjogu chased him up to the Chichagi River (River Oti), by then it was late in the evening as Naa Sulugu had crossed the river. So Dakpam Naa Kpanjogu and his men slept at the riverbank overnight.

The following morning, Dakpam Naa crossed the river, and they continued the fight. According to oral tradition, they fought for five days until when they got to the mountains at Jarikpan in the present-day Republic of Togo, Naa Sulgu's horse became exhausted and could no longer climb the mountains and Dakpam Naa Kpanjogu met him there and killed him. Naa Sulgu was buried at Jarikpan and not in Bimbilla (*Oral Literature of Late Bimbilla Lung-Naa Alhaji Abdulai, 2008*).

After Dakpam Naa Kpanjogu succeeded Naa Sulgu in the fight, he asked of Nakpaa Naa Azuma. He was informed that Nakpaa Naa Azuma was in the Bassari Land and had heard of the fight between him and Naa Sulgu. Nakpaa Naa Azuma was found and Dakpam Naa Kpanjogu told him: "*I have done so many investigations and was well informed that, I will succeed Naa Sulgu in the fight. Secondly, that I should allow you (Nakpaa Naa Azuma) to be enskinned as Bimbilla Naa, so prepare for Bimbilla throne*". Having finished the funeral of the late Naa Damba, Nakpaa Naa Azuma resisted that, the uncle wanted to deceive him and killed him on the Bimbilla skin. Dakpam Naa Kpanjogu said again "*you should also go and conduct your own investigations to confirm whether what I am telling you is the truth or not. He added, if I become the Bimbilla Naa you cannot provide me the needed security and Naa Sulgu's family will prepare to attack us and they will succeed us forever, but when you become Bimbilla Naa, I can be in Dakpam and provide you the needed security, so that the Bimbilla skin/title will remain for your children and my children forever. No more blood will be shed*". Nakpaa Naa Azuma was convinced and accepted the Bimbilla skin/

title. However, before the enskinment, both of them took an oath of succession to the Bimbilla Title/Skin; (Nam) that, after Naa Azuma (Naa Gbuguma) from the Nakpaa Title, my son or younger brother from Dakpam title shall be the next Bimbilla Naa. And it shall continue in this rotational manner. Under no circumstance shall Nakpaa Title or Dakpam Title be enskinned on Bimbilla Skin/Title on two consecutive times or more. It shall be rotational between Nakpaa and Dakpam Titles. The oath they took consists of the Gbewaa Skins (Power of Authority) and the Holy Quran, which was added by Malam Mahama Walji. This marked the beginning of Bang-yili and Gbuguma-yili rotational gates system in the 16th century. In recognition of the role Malam Mahama Walji played, Dakpam Naa Kpanjogu requested he should remain in Bimbilla to help them rule Nanung and honoured as the Chief Imam of Nanung kingdom. As such, he was enskinned as the first Chief Imam of Bimbilla. Hence, Malam Mahama Walji started the Bimbilla Chief Imam's Title. Chief Imam Amidu, Chief Imam Kassim just to mention a few are the real family of Chief Imam Mahama Walji. One of the family members even named his hotel in Tamale after their grandfather called Walji Lodge, located around Russia Bungalow in Tamale, Northern Region. The two royal gates of Nanung (Gbuguma-yili & Bang-yili) are descendants of Naa Nyelinbolgu. Below are the rotational gate titles:

# 3.1 Gbuguma-yili Royal Gate.

| Title | Village/Town |
|---|---|
| Nakpaa – Naa Most Senior Title | Nakpaa |
| Bakpaba – Naa Second Senior Title | Bakpaba |
| Karaga – Lana | Kalgah |
| Jua – Naa | Jua |
| Lepusi– Naa | Lepuhi |
| Gundow – Naa | Gundoo |
| Lanja – Naa | Langja |
| Boyu – Naa | Makayili |
| Yayiri – Lana | Yayiriya |
| Nating – Lana | Natiŋa |
| Banvim – Lana | Banvim |
| Suya – Naa | Kabulya |
| Yamo | Yamo |
| Mion. | Mion/Jagbuni |

According to oral literature, Nakpaa and Bakpaba follow each other in terms of seniority; the rest of the titles beginning from Karaga can overlap each other in succession to Bakpaba and Nakpaa titles. In addition, if a male son from the Gbuguma-yili gate is holding Lanja title, he can aspire to other titles such as Lepusi-Naa, Jua-Naa, Gundow-Naa, Bakpaba-Naa and Nakpaa-Naa. However, if a Princess's son or an ordinary person is holding the Lanja title, he cannot aspire to any of the above-mentioned titles. Princess's sons or ordinary persons are strictly limited to Lanja. Yamo and Mion are old communities and for that, matter titles since Naa Gmantambu came to Nanung. New communities have progressed over them repeatedly, making these communities/titles to remain backwards in succession and progression. These communities/titles eventually became titles for elders in the Gbuguma-yili Royal gate and can no longer aspire to other titles.

## 3.2 Bang-yili Royal Gate Titles.

| Title | Village/Town |
|---|---|
| Dakpam-Naa; Most Senior | Dakpam |
| Chamba-Naa; Second | Chamba |
| Gbungbalga-Naa; Third | Gbumgbalga |
| Lungni-Naa | Lungni |
| Sakpe-Naa | Sakpe |
| Gimam-Naa | Jimam |
| Tuu-Naa | Tuu |
| Kukuo-Naa | Nassamba-Kukuo |
| Kpaluhi-Naa | Kpaluhi |
| Sikpam-Naa | Sikpam |
| Nassamba-Naa | Nasamba |
| Chirifa –Naa | Chirifa |

From Gbungbalga, the rest of the titles can also overlap each other to the three senior titles. Chirifa is one of the oldest community/titles. Due to succession and progression by some of the new communities/titles, it has remained back and is now regarded as elder's title. Previously, with Chirifa title you could aspire to other titles.

Since they took the oath of succession to the Bimbilla Skin/Title, succession to Bimbilla Skin/Title has been rotational and very successful upon several attempts by some few individuals who tried to use different titles to the Bimbilla Skin/Title in the presence of Nakpaa and Dakpam titles *(Oral Literature of Late Bimbilla Lung-Naa Alhaji Abdulai, 2008)*.


## 3.3 Queen Mothers.


### 3.3.1 Bang-yili Royal Gate:

❖ Kpaliga Ponaa (Queen-Mother of Kpalga near Bimbilla)

❖ Nakpaanzou Naa (Queen-Mother)

❖

### 3.3.2 Gbuguma-yili Royal Gate:

❖ Gikuhi Ponaa (Queen-Mother)

❖ Kuɣlogu Lana (Queen-Mother)

❖ Shilin Naa (Queen-Mother)

❖ Kpatuya (Queen-Mother)

## 3.4 Succession Disputes.

The rotational gate system has experienced some succession disputes since its inception. Notable among them are as follows:

Naa Yakubu Savigu (*Savi'suŋ ni laɣim kuruti, Gampilisuŋ ni laɣim niriba*) was the twenty second chief of Bimbilla. However, there was a very serious misunderstanding before Naa Yakubu Savigu was enskinned. It came because of Bakpaba-Naa Iddrisa who wanted to use Bakpaba Title to Bimbilla when Nakpaa-Naa was there. Bakpaba-Naa Iddrisa was driven away because of a conflict between him and Naa Peinkpaa. The conflict arose when Naa Peinkpaa prepared Bakpaba-Naa Iddrisa and sent him to support his brother "Yaa Naa Abdulai Naɣibiegu" in the fight against Baassaris in the 18th century *(according to the genealogy of Yani chiefs)*. After Bakpaba-Naa Iddrisa successfully fought for "Yaa Naa Abdulai Naɣibiegu" in the Baassari conflict, he was convinced that, he could succeed Naa Peinkpaa and become the Bimbilla Naa, which was not possible. As a result, he went and settled around Krachi. Before he returned to Bakpaba, one of his younger brothers (Naa Yakubu Savigu) from the Gbuguma-yili gate had progressed to Nakpaa. After the death of Naa Toli (Naa Dahamani) from Bang-yili, Bakpaba-Naa Iddrisa wanted to use power over Nakpaa-Naa Yakubu Savigu. Juo Naa said, "I could not give it to you because there is an oath in Nakpaa and Dakpam over Bimbilla succession". Bakpaba-Naa Iddrisa said Juo Naa should prepare for an attack if he is not going to be the one to be enskinned. The very day Juo Naa scheduled for the enskinment of Naa Yakubu Savigu, it could not come on because Bakpaba-Naa Iddrisa threatened to attack. A meeting was summoned by Juo Naa to inform the elders of Nanung the reason why the enskinment could not come on. Dakpam Naa Bukari asked: *is it true Bakpaba-Naa Iddrisa actually said it?* The answer was **'yes'** by Bakpaba-Naa Iddrisa. Dakpam Naa Bukari said "*N-yaba Juo Naa, get prepared tonight to perform your function, enskinment of Bimbilla Naa, Bakpaba-Naa Iddrisa prepare very well, and we shall see who is who*". Indeed, Naa Yakubu was enskinned successfully without any interference by Bakpaba-Naa Iddrisa. Again, Bakpaba-Naa Iddrisa went back to Krachi area, Banda to be precise and as such the founder of the present-day Banda community in the Kpandai District. Some few months after the enskinment of Naa Yakubu Savigu, Bakpaba-Naa Iddrisa came back vigorously with an attack and killed Naa Yakubu Savigu. Dakpam Naa Bukari said he would never call Bakpaba-Naa Iddrisa his father "Bimbilla Naa". He also got prepared and attacked Backpaba-Naa Iddrisa and killed him around Kpatinga area specifically known as *walinpaw-ni*. The mysterious death of Bakpaba-Naa Iddrisa gave rise to the existence of two Gods "Chebto ancient pots & Shrine and Pinaa Shrine & Cave". These historic landmarks are very important sites for the development of tourism *(Oral Literature of Late Bimbilla Lung-Naa Alhaji Abdulai and Kpatinga Tindana, 2008).*

After Dakpam Naa Bukari killed Bakpaba-Naa Iddrisa, it was the turn of Dakpam Naa Bukari to be enskinned as Bimbilla Naa. He said, *"I would not sit on this burnt and smoking skins of Bimbilla"*. As such, he has wholeheartedly given this chance to the Uncle Naa Wahu (Naa Abalsi) who was then the Chamba Naa. Juo Naa said even though you have openly given this chance to your uncle, but it will still go against the oath of Bimbilla skin succession. Dakpam Naa Bukari maintained that it should be given to his Uncle and Juo Naa said then do it yourself, because I will not do it myself to cause a problem for the people of Juo. After a proper understanding was reached, Naa Wahu was enskinned as Bimbilla Naa by Juo Naa, and he was the twenty-third chief of Bimbilla.

The Nanumba and German war occurred during the term of Naa Wahu in 1898. Naa Wahu ruled Nanung for 35 years (1890 – 1925). Naa Wahu appellations were *"Kundung Kurili lu kpaha ka kundun-bihi wari waa; Laamihi dapali ban kaɣizali ni gurigi, Abarika dapali ban ti suɣa ni me ya; Dakuɣu din daŋ duu ni kari wori"*, meaning; "old wolf fell sick, and the young ones are jubilating; those who are well prepared shall be disorganized; the one who erects thatch structures shall build mansions; and the first firewood that enters the room shall warm the body".

*Naa Ziblim Kuntibsa*

Naa Ziblim Kuntibsa was the twenty-fourth chief of Bimbilla, followed by Naa Mahami who the twenty-fifth chief of Bimbilla was. Naa Salifu should have been the twenty-fifth chief of Bimbilla but he was arrested and detained by the Germans due to certain issues. As such, the German Governor asked for the one who was next to Naa Salifu, to be enskinned. Naa Mahami was the one next to him from Gbungbalga. He was enskinned as a provisional chief because Naa Salifu was alive. According to the custom and tradition of Nanung, until a chief is dead and ritual funeral (Nakuli) had been performed, which is the only condition for succession, the customary alternation between the two-gate system was not permissible. No Nanumba chief has been disskinned *(The Judicial Committee of the Nanumba Traditional Council Judgement, 2003)*. After Naa Mahami, Naa Haruna was next on the skin of Bimbilla as the twenty-sixth chief. However, there was a problem here too. By then, the Germans were governing the eastern corridor previously known as the Trans-volta Togo land. They were based in Krachi and sent a delegation to witness the performance of Bimbilla Naa Mahami's funeral. Before they started the funeral, they sent for the then Nakpaa Naa (Nakpaa Naa Attah, son of Bimbilla Naa Shero) and he refused. After the funeral, again, they sent for Nakpaa Naa Attah with some of the German Governor's delegation and again he refused. The German Governor asked the elders who represented the Nakpaa Naa Attah and performed the funeral. The elders said Bakpaba-Naa Haruna, and the Governor said he should be enskinned as Bimbilla Naa. Juo Naa resisted and said he does not want to go against the Bimbilla succession oath. The Governor asked Bakpaba-Naa Haruna what instructions your elder brother (Nakpaa Naa Attah) gave to you. He said, "I should do all that is necessary on his behalf". It was finally resolved that, Bakpaba-Naa Haruna should be given the nod on behalf of his elder brother "Nakpaa Naa Attah" and that at any point his elder brother expressed interest, he should hand over to him. This was how Bakpaba-Naa Haruna used Bakpaba title to Bimbilla skin. According to some old school of oral literature, Nakpaa Naa Attah's daughter was seriously sick and when he tried to prepare and come to Bimbilla for the title, his wife provoked him by saying: *"your daughter is seriously sick, and you do not care rather anxious for Bimbilla skin title"*. That was the reason why he could not come for the title.

According to the late Bimbilla-Lung-Naa Alhaji Abdulai, after Naa Haruna, Naa Salifu was returned to the skin of Bimbilla based upon consultation with the then Dakpam

Naa Attah who openly obliged Naa Salifu to come and continue. When the Germans at Krachi released him from detention and the rotation had come to the turn of Bang-yili gate, the elders thought it prudent for Naa Salifu to continue. Naa Salifu was the twenty-seventh chief of Bimbilla as such, they appellated him as: "*Nama say 'kurili; Na' ŋuni min di nam ka zaŋ zali bieɣuni n-lahi di?*

He also indicated that Naa Abdulai Kurugu-kpaa was next on the skin of Bimbilla and he was the twenty-eighth chief of Bimbilla. Naa Abdulai Kurugu-Kpaa ruled Nanung for 18 years (1926 – 1944). After Naa Abdulai Kurugu-kpaa, Naa Natogmah II was the twenty-ninth chief of Bimbilla. Dakpam Naa Dadinkai missed the Bimbilla skin shortly within some few days by death. He was a great-grand son of Naa Peinkpaa. Dakpam Naa Bukari was the son (Regent) of Naa Peinkpaa. Dakpam Naa Bukari gave birth to Nabiyong (prince) Adam and he gave birth to Dakpam Naa Daadinkai.

*Naa Natogmah Attah II (1944 – 1959)*

Naa Natogmah had the opportunity and used Gbungbalga title to the Bimbilla skin. He ruled Nanung for 15 years (1944 – 1959).

*Naa Dassana Abdulai (1959 – 1981*

Naa Dassana became the thirtieth chief of Bimbilla. There was another misunderstanding between Nakpaa Naa Dassana and Bakpaba-Naa Dawuni. That is, Bakpaba-Naa Dawuni claimed that, by birth, he was the eldest person in Gbuguma-yili gate, whiles Nakpaa Naa Dassana by chieftaincy title was the senior-most in the gate. The succession issue was resolved with the intervention of the Northern Regional Commissioner Mr. R. R. Abavana, based on the rotational gate system (Dakpam & Nakpaa) titles. With this, Nakpaa Naa is the one who qualifies to be enskinned as Bimbilla Naa. After Naa Dassana was enskinned, he gave Nakpaa title to Bakpaba-Naa Dawuni and Bakpaba title to the regent of Naa Natogmah. The Bakpaba title was a misplaced title for the regent of Naa Natogmah II, because it is not the Naa Bang-yili gate system title which has never happened according to the custom and tradition of Nanung. Naa Dassana ruled Nanung for 22 years (1959 – 1981). His appellations were: *"Gbungbun turi babli, dab'ayi ni ata, babli bliya"*.

*Bimbilla Naa Abarika Attah II (1983 – 1999)*

Naa Abarika Attah II was the thirty-one chief of Bimbilla. History has repeated in the Naa Bang-yili royal gate. Naa Natogmah II and Naa Abarika II were the same mother and the same father like in the case of Naa Pienkpaa and Naa Toli. This is a unique historic event in Naa Bang-yili and Nanung. It has never happened in Dagbon or Mamprugu. Naa Abarika II ruled Nanung for 16 years (1983 – 1999). Naa Abarika appellations were "Gbanbeigu, so yipri so yoyim mo" meaning; "a strong skin, you will disturb it and leave it, if somebody misbehave him/her was influenced by another person".


From the above succession cases of the rotational gate system, had repeatedly occurred only in the Gbuguma-yili gate. But the rhetorical question is: why only Gbuguma-yili gate system? Is it that they are not respecting the gate system titles? The current succession case has lasted for about a decade and beyond between Nakpaa Naa Alhaji Salifu Dawuni and Mr. Andani Dassana Abdulai. Also, with careful readings of the above succession cases, there were all resolved in favour of Nakpaa's title with the basic principles of the rotational gate system (Dakpam & Nakpaa) titles. Except in some few cases where the Dakpam Naa or Nakpaa Naa openly obliged for the next title to succeed upon serious scrutiny by Juo Naa. It is very clear from all the succession cases above that no other title contested with Dakpam title or Nakpaa title and won the case. Why with this millennium era and globalization engulfed with some negative characters who, under the guise of some political portfolios, bureaucratically mare the reputation of some national institutions like the

National House of Chiefs' judicial committee to commit the blander of destroying the whole Nanung kingdom customary practices and tradition evidenced by the 8th of October 2014 judgment on the Bimbilla chieftaincy appeal?

# CHAPTER 4

## BIMBILLA CHIEFTAINCY CONFLICT.

### 4.0 The Genesis of Bimbilla Chieftaincy Conflict.

The Yani Skin *"Nam"* succession conflict that has bedeviled Dagbon repeatedly has been transmitted to the Bimbilla skin *"Nam"*. The Bimbilla skin "Nam" succession dispute between the two factions in the Gbuguma-yili royal gate emerged prematurely during the reign of the late Bimbilla Naa Abarika Attah II of the Bang-yili royal gate, when some particular family lines of the Gbuguma-yili gate continued to ignore the Bakpaba title for fear of death as there is a curse invoked on the skin. This phenomenon led to the prolonged vacant title of Bakpaba, which was a very worrying issue to the late Bimbilla Naa Abarika Attah II. In an attempt to fill the vacant Bakpaba title, Naa Abarika Attah requested the elders of the Gbuguma-yili gate to identify their leader to come for the Bakpaba's title. This request was sent several times and the elders turned it down since 1985. Later the current Nakpaa-Naa Salifu Dawuni bid for the Bakpaba's title in 1986 and successfully got the title. The belief was that he would die on the Bakpaba skin as the curse holds. As such, no body from Gbuguma-yili gate challenged him on the Bakpaba title but rather, he was supported by members of the Gbuguma-Yili royal gate to go ahead with his bidding. According to the gate system of Gbuguma-yili, Bakpaba title is next to Nakpaa. However, when Nakpaa title became vacant in the late 1980s, the late Naa Abarika Attah denied Bakpaba-Naa Salifu Dawuni for the first time and gave the Nakpaa title to the late Nakpaa-Naa Musah Abdulai (son of Bimbilla-Naa Abdulai & younger brother of Bimbilla-Naa Dassana Abdulai).

After the death of Nakpaa Naa Musah Abdulai, the late Naa Abarika Attah enskinned Bakpaba-Naa Salifu Dawuni as Nakpaa-Naa on the 26th of March 1992 *(CV of Nakpaa-Naa Alhaji Salifu Dawuni)*. Immediately after his enskinment a group of people from Gbuguma-yili led by Kpatihi Naa Ponadoo filed a petition challenging Naa Abarika Attah II for the enskinment of Nakpaa-Naa Salifu Dawuni as a great grandson at the Northern Region House of Chiefs. The case was ruled in favour of the defendants herein referred to as (Naa Abarika Attah II & Nakpaa Salifu Dawuni). They were not satisfied with the ruling by the Judicial Committee of the Northern Regional House of Chiefs and again filed an appeal at the Chieftaincy Tribunal of the National House of Chiefs Appeal Court in Kumasi. The case was struck out with ¢500,000.00 (old Cedis) cost to both respondents for want of prosecution *(In the Chieftaincy Tribunal of the National House of Chiefs Appeal Court, Kumasi sitting on Thursday 12th February 1998).*

The event of the Bimbilla chieftaincy crisis got to its turning point after the funeral of the late Bimbilla Naa Abarika Attah II in March 2003. Before the funeral, the Northern Regional Security Committee (REGSEC) convened a meeting with kingmakers and other opinion leaders to sign an undertaking that, there shall not be confusion about succession to the Bimbilla skin. All parties signed the undertaking before RESEC gave an approval for the funeral of the late Naa Abarika Attah II was performed. Immediately after the funeral, REGSEC gave an order to suspend the enskinment process of the current Nakpaa Naa before they deal with the security issues. The head of the kingmakers (Juo Regent, Osman Mahama acting in the capacity of Juo Naa after the power vested in him as acting-Juo Naa by the late paramount chief of Bimbilla Naa Abarika Attah II) respected the order of REGSEC for the period. Whiles Juo Regent was waiting for the order from REGSEC, one Azumah Nantogmah ignored the order by REGSEC and secretly and uncustomary enskinned one Andani Dassana as Bimbilla-Naa. Juo Regent customarily nullified the installation of Mr. Andani Dassana by Azumah Nantogmah. Juo Regent summoned an emergency meeting with the Kingmakers of the Chiefdom. Juo Regent, upon consultation with the Kingmakers, followed the due process and enskinned Nakpaa-Naa Alhaji Salifu Dawuni as Bimbilla Naa after the judgment by the Nanumba Traditional Council Judicial Committee on the 29th day of July 2003. This gave birth to factions in Nanung as such they were two rival chiefs in Bimbilla.

The Nanumba Traditional Council in collaboration with the District Security Committee (DISEC) formed a judicial committee known as 'Gumah Commission' in 2003 to look into the Bimbilla Skin succession dispute. "The commission findings were:

- ❖ Juo Naa is the head of Kingmakers according to the custom of Nanung.

- ❖ Juo Naa is solely responsible for the appointment of Bimbilla-Naa.

- ❖ Juo Naa takes custody of the regalia.

- ❖ They are two gate system (Gbuguma-yili and Bang-yili).

- ❖ The gate system is rotational based on the gate skin titles (Nakpaa and Dakpam).

- ❖ **The succession to Bimbilla skin does not restrict grandsons or great grandsons, provided one aspire to Nakpaa or Dakpam based on the rotation of the gate system".**

As such, the Judicial Committee confirmed the appointment made by Juo Regent Osman Mahama as legitimate. Politicians frustrated the efforts of the Judicial Committee, and the issue again aggravated. The Nanung dilemma propelled astray when the overlord of Mamprugu Traditional area, Nayiri (Naa Bohagu Mahami Abdulai II) who, with inadequate investigation into the matter, pronounced judgment in favour of Andani Dassana. A good number of Nanung opinion leaders suspected foul play at Mamprugu. As a result, Naa Salifu Dawuni and Juo Regent (Osman Mahama) filed a petition on February 10, 2004 contending that the 1st petitioner (Naa Salifu Dawuni) is the rightful person to occupy the Bimbilla skin as Bimbilla Naa to the Judicial Committee of the Northern Regional House of Chiefs, Tamale. The petition to the Judicial Committee of the Northern Regional House of Chiefs by Naa Salifu Dawuni and Juo Regent (Osman Mahama) is as follows:

*Bimbilla Naa Salifu Dawuni (1st petitioner) and Juo Regent Osman Mahama (2nd petitioner) filed a petition on 10th February 2004. The petitioners are contending that the 1st petitioner (Bimbilla Naa Salifu Dawuni) is the rightful person to occupy the Bimbilla Skin as Bimbilla-Naa and acting in that capacity are claiming against the defendants the following reliefs:*

> (i) *Declaration that the 1st petitioner is the Bimbilla-Naa duly nominated and enskinned in accordance with the Nanung custom.*

> (ii) *Declaration that the 2nd petitioner is the sole authority to nominate a candidate for enskinment as Bimbilla-Naa.*

> (iii) *Declaration that the purported nomination of the 1st petitioner by 2nd petitioner and the subsequent purported enskinment of 1st petitioner as Bimbilla-Naa are nullities.*

(iv) *Declaration that the 2^nd defendant (Azumah Nantogmah) is not a kingmaker within the Nanung custom and is also not a Regent of Kpatihi-Naa."*

The case lasted for 8 years (2004 – 2012) with the Judicial Committee of the Northern Regional House of Chiefs, Tamale. On 13th March 2012, the Judicial Committee passed judgment, which they deemed *unanimous decision* of the committee in favour of Andani Dassana (1st defendant) and Azumah Nantogmah (2nd defendant). The judgment was based on the following findings:

> *"The committee after thorough evaluation of the evidence adduced by the parties finds that the 1st petitioner has no capacity to bring this action to the committee under the erroneous title of Bimbilla-Naa, a title which he does not hold in accordance with the findings of the committee.*
>
> *First, the consent of the Gbuguma-yili family from where he the 1st petitioner hails **which should have entitled him** to be put forward was not sought. The family did not only show or express its discontent for this apparent lack of consultation by those who erroneously nominated him. In fact, his family did not choose him but rather rejected him and nominated another candidate who is the 1st defendant in the person of Andani Dassana.*

*Secondly, he has been declared a great grandson and also from the maternal line by his family and the majority of the kingmakers and therefore the Northern Regional Judicial Committee found that the 1<sup>st</sup> petitioner is not qualified to become Bimbilla Naa under the relevant Nanung customs and the chieftaincy Laws of Ghana.*

*Thirdly, the 1<sup>st</sup> petitioner Salifu Dawuni was not properly elected. His faulty election by which he is relying on as Bimbilla Naa was done by a minority of the kingmakers an act which is against legal principles particularly case of Law and also against the democratic principles established in Ghana.*

*Again, the nomination of the 1<sup>st</sup> petitioner was further found irregular and faulty when one single individual called Juo Regent single-handedly nominated him without seeking the consent of his family. That the said individual arbitrarily declared that he alone could put forward the 1<sup>st</sup> petitioner as Bimbilla Naa even without the participation of any other kingmakers if he wished so to do. In exercising this wide power, the 2<sup>nd</sup> petitioner claims he was exercising his powers under Nanung custom. This committee however finds that such a custom, which will empower an individual to act in this manner, is not only* *repugnant to the principles of equity, good conscience, and natural justice but also contrary to the accepted principles, which our courts have accepted when determining customary Law in respect of chieftaincy disputes.*

*The committee finds that since the 2nd petitioner, the Juo Regent (Osman Mahama) has tied himself to the apron string of the 1st petitioner, his downfall means he the 2nd petitioner cannot also stand.*

*The final issue, which this committee is being called upon to determine, is whether the petitioners are entitled to their reliefs.*

*The committee in order to give brief but comprehensive explanations will deal with these reliefs one by one. Starting with the Declaration that 1st petitioner is Bimbilla Naa duly nominated and enskinned, the committee rejects this assertion on the grounds which had been already indicated in this judgment in details. However, it will not be misplaced if the committee says that the 1st petitioner's nomination was faulty. His election being done by the minority of the kingmakers cannot be sustained. His enskinment rites, which were done by Worikpomo instead of Kpatihi Regent, infringed the Nanung custom of enskinment. This fact established when his own witness PW2 told the committee that the enskinment rites on Bimbilla Naas are the responsibility of Kpatihi family.*

*The committee after thorough evaluation of the evidence on record in respect of the 2nd Declaration that the 2nd petition is the sole authority to nominate a candidate for enskinment as Bimbilla Naa, the committee unanimously refused to accept this claim on the grounds that if the 2nd petitioner is authorized by custom to nominate and elect as a sole individual such a custom is bad and cannot stand in view of known Legal principles particularly case Law in Ghana. The failure of the 2nd petitioner to seek the consent and concurrence of the family of the 1st petitioner is a testimony that his so-called power to nominate as a sole person or individual and whatever he had done there under to purportedly make 1st petitioner Bimbilla Naa is a Nullity.*

*The invitation to the Northern Regional Judicial committee to declare that the purported nomination of the 1st defendant by the 2nd defendant and the subsequent purported enskinment of the 2nd defendant as Bimbilla Naa are Nullities **is a wrong invitation because the 1st defendant evidentially was nominated effectively by his family who handed him over to the kingmakers through the 2nd defendant.***

*Furthermore, the 1ˢᵗ defendant was validly elected by the majority of the kingmakers of Nanung in accordance with Nanung custom and legal principles.*

*In addition to this enskinment rites were performed on the 1ˢᵗ defendant by acting Kpatihi Regent of Kpatihi family in the person of the 2ⁿᵈ defendant Azumah Nantogmah who has been declared by this judgment as the acting Kpatihi Regent. The Kpatihi family is the family the petitioners' own witness PWI admitted being responsible for the performance of enskinment rites on Bimbilla Naas. It goes on and on.*

*The committee having considered the absolute weaknesses of the petitioner's case in respect of the various issues, especially the inconsistencies and conflicts their pieces of evidence exposed as against the formidable case presented by the defense, hereby refused to grant the petitioners the reliefs they are seeking from the committee as the petitioners are not entitled to any of the said reliefs".*

*The above listed findings by the Judicial Committee of the Northern Regional House of Chiefs on which basis the judgment was passed against the 1ˢᵗ and 2ⁿᵈ petitioners is very ridiculous and biased on the grounds as follows:*

That the consent of the Gbuguma-yili family from where he the 1ˢᵗ petitioner hails which should have entitled him to be put forward was not sought. According to the custom of Nanung, succession to the Bimbilla skin title is based on the gate-system title in accordance with the rotational gate system (Gbuguma-yili & Bang-yili) as defined by the custom of Nanung. Consultations are done at the time every young prince begins the gate system titles. It is at this stage family consultations play a very important role. Some particular family lines of the Gbuguma-yili gate continue to ignore Bakpaba's title for fear of death, as it was a curse. This phenomenon led to the prolonged vacant title of Bakpaba, which was a very worrying issue to the late Bimbilla Naa Abarika Attah II. In an attempt to fill the vacant Bakpaba title, Naa Abarika Attah requested the elders of the Gbuguma-yili gate to identify their leader to come for the Bakpaba's title. This request was sent several times and the elders turned it down in 1985. Later, the current Nakpaa-Naa Salifu Dawuni came for the Bakpaba's title in 1986 (*CV of Nakpaa Naa Salifu Dawuni*). The belief was that he would die on the Bakpaba title as the curse holds. As such, nobody challenged him on the Bakpaba's title. The progression of a prince to Nakpaa or Dakpam is an automatic continuous assessment of his credibility to lead the gate to the ultimate title 'Bimbilla skin title'. Once a sitting Bimbilla Naa dies, depending on the rotation of the gate system, Dakpam and Nakpaa are automatic to succeed the vacant Bimbilla skin title.

Juo Naa does not nominate a candidate according to the custom of Nanung but atomically select either Dakpam

Naa or Nakpaa Naa depending on the royal gate that has just ended it turn. The selected candidate is notified by a presentation of cola-nuts to inform him that he has elevated to the ultimate title of the land (Overload of Nanung). The Judicial Committee of the Northern Region House of Chiefs has wrongly defined the functions and powers of Juo Naa so far as the custom and tradition of Nanung is concerned. **It is important to make it clear to the public that according to Nanung custom, Juo Naa is the vice president of the Nanumba Traditional Council. As soon as the Bimbilla Naa passes away, he becomes the head of Nanung until the ritual funeral "Nakuli" is performed. After which he select the next Bimbilla Naa and hands over to him. Juo Naa is also the head of the kingmakers who takes custody of the regalia** *(for more information on the powers of Juo Naa refers to chapter 2 of this book).* **Juo Naa Dawuni was the one who gave the regalia to Kpatihi Naa when wild animals drove away the inhabitants of Juo to Jakpafili to keep it as a caretaker** *(The Judicial Committee of the Nanumba Traditional Council Judgement, 2003).* **Today, it is very interesting caretakers are claiming custody of the regalia. Naa Gmantambu mandated Juo Naa to take custody of the regalia, select and perform the enskinment rites of Bimbilla Naa**. Nabang Tindana, now known and called Juo Naa was the head of the Tindamba in Nanung when Naa Gmantambu arrived in Nanung in the late 14th century. Among the Tindamba were: Daalana, Sirikpomo Tindana, Suburi Tindana, Kpandigli Ponaa, Kpandigli Ponadow, Varili (Jilo) Tindana, Lanjiri (Kukuo) Tindana, Wunpigu (Tagnamo) Tindana and Naban (Juo) Tindana. As the number of the kingmakers increased, Juo Naa delegated some of the functions such as, performance of enskinment rites to Gambuga Naa and Lanjiri Naa. The core function of **Kpatihi** according to the custom of Nanung is protocol duty responsible for serving food to visitors during festivals such as Damba. It is for this reason the legends or Tomtom Beaters praises Kpatihi Naas as *"Sahi yara naa"* meaning *a chief responsible for serving food.* Our custom is derived from the oral tradition and the Tomtom Beaters who are the legends hold this oral tradition. Later Kpatihi Naa was co-opted into the members of kingmakers to perform delegator's function by Gambuga Naa and Lanjiri Naa *(Oral Literature of Bimbilla Lung-Naa Alhaj Abdulai, 2008).*


According to oral literature, before Naa Gbuguma, one could use any title to Bimbilla skin title. The very last chief who used Suburi title to Bimbilla skin title was Naa Sulgu (Son of Naa Mahamudu or Wobgu) from the Suburi family of Bimbilla succeeded Naa Damba through a fight and became Bimbilla Naa. 13 chiefs succeeded Bimbilla skin title before the rotational gate system. Below were the chiefs:

1. Naa Gmantambu, son of Naa Gbewaa
2. Naa Sulgme
3. Naa Kumkayoɣri, son of Gmantambu
4. Naa Dogiporigu, son of Sulgme

5. Naa Badariga
6. Naa Naɣi Baarigu
7. Naa Saa
8. Naa Koŋa
9. Naa Kunbalinkulga
10. Naa Nyelinbolgu, son of Kunbalinkulga
11. Naa Wobgu (Naa Pampamli or Mahamudu)
12. Naa Saa-kpang (Naa Damba) son of Nyelinbolgu
13. Naa Sulgu (Naa Maamani), son of Wobgu/Mahamuda

According to oral literature, Naa Sulgu succeeded Naa Damba through an attack. Dakpam Naa Kpanjogu was the younger brother of Naa Damba. Nakpaa Naa Azumah (Naa Gbuguma) uncle was Naa Damba. As such, Naa Sulgu extended the fight to Dakpam and Nakpaa and drove them away. Later, Dakpam Naa Kpanjogu came back to Dakpam and resettled. Bimbilla-Chichagi road and Bimbilla-Salaga road were among the Trans-Sahara routes for slave trade by the Arab Slave-traders and other traders from Nigeria, Togo, and Saudi Arabia among others, used for trade during the ancient times (*the slave mosques can be found in the present day Laribanga near Korili (Nakpaali), Chichagi and Kpalga near Bimbilla and communities along the route*). There was a Hausa man called Mahama Walji who was engaged in cattle and cola-nut trade from Ghana to Nigeria. During this period, he was passing through Bimbilla with his animals and Naa Sulgu ordered his people to kill the animals. The second batch of his animals was killed in Bimbilla. The man got to Dakpam; his usual resting place and linked up with Dakpam Naa Kpanjogu where he supported him with spiritual preparation from the Holy Quran to fight Naa Sulgu. Indeed, when Naa Sulgu and his men attacked him, he succeeded Naa Sulgu. After the fight Dakpam Naa Kpanjogu told Nakpaa Naa Azumah to occupy, the Bimbilla skin title, so that he will be outside providing him with security. After him, his son who occupies Dakpam will become the next Bimbilla Naa. An agreement was reached between the two and they took an oath of succession to the Bimbilla skin title with the Gbewaa skins and the Holy Quran, which Mahama Walji added to the skins. They swore to rule/enskin as Bimbilla Naa one after the other and that in no instance shall one particular gate rule/ enskin on two consecutive times or more. In addition, no one from any of the royal gates shall use his name or any other title apart from Dakpam and Nakpaa. It is highly prohibited to go against this traditional oath of succession to Bimbilla Skin/Title "Nam". This was how the rotational gate system (Gbuguma-yili & Bang-yili) of Nanung chiefdom evolved. Since the rotational gate system was instituted in the custom of Nanung, succession to the Bimbilla skin title has been based on the two rotational gate system with Nakpaa and Dakpam being used to occupy the Bimbilla Skin title. As such, it is the latest transition according to the custom and tradition of Nanung for more than two centuries now. No prince had used his name to succeed Bimbilla skin title. (*For more information, refer to chapter 3 of this book.*)


History has repeated itself in the Gbuguma-yili royal gate of Nanung rotational gate system. Succession dispute repeatedly occurs in only the Gbuguma-yili royal gate and this current one between Nakpaa-Naa Alhaji Salifu Dawuni and Andani Dassana is the third time. The previous two were between **Bakpaba-Naa Iddrisa verses Nakpaa-Naa Yakubu (Bimbilla Naa Yakubu Savigu)** and **Bakpaba-Naa Dawuni verses Nakpaa-Naa Dassana Abdulai (Bimbilla Naa Dassana Abdulai)**. The two succession disputes were resolved based on the rotational gate system of Nanung that is between Dakpam and Nakpaa titles. The 1$^{st}$ defendant's father "Naa Dassana Abdulai" became Bimbilla Naa over Bakpaba Naa Dawuni because of the rotational gate system. In the same vein, Nakpaa-Naa Yakubu also became Bimbilla Naa over Bakpaba-Naa Iddrisa. However, in some special circumstances, one can use other titles such as Bakpaba, Jua, Gbungbalga, Chamba among others depending on the situation to Bimbilla skin title. This is to explain when Nakpaa or Dakpam title's falls vacant. Another condition is when the Nakpaa Naa/Dakpam Naa may oblige for the next with lesser tittle to succeed Bimbills skin upon serious scrutiny by the Juo Naa. Except these conditions above, no royal with lesser title could bypass Dakpam or Nakpaa titles to succeed Bimbilla Skin title. For example, Dakpam Naa Bukari and Chamba Naa Abalsi (Bimbilla Naa Wahu) from Bang-yili gate and Nakpaa Naa Attah and Bakpaba Naa Haruna (Bimbilla Naa Haruna) from Gbuguma-yili gate. *For more information, refer to chapter*

Furthermore, if the purported nomination and enskinment of the 1ˢᵗ petitioner was erroneous and faulty on the grounds that Kpatihi Naa or acting Kpatihi did not perform the enskinment rites as the committee holds as a fact, then the nomination and enskinment of Naa Abdulai (1ˢᵗ defendant's grandfather) was also erroneous and faulty. **Because he was in the same way nominated by, Juo Naa and Warikpomo performed his enskinment rites**. However, the most appropriate word according to Nanung custom is either **selected** or **appointed** by Juo Naa. This implies that the 1ˢᵗ defendant and his father "Naa Dassana Abdulai" were not qualified to contest the Bimbilla skin title or become Bimbilla Naa. In addition, the same erroneous and faulty enskinment applies to 11 Bimbilla chiefs. They include the following:

1. Naa Natogmah I (Naa Peinkpaa), son of Naa Abarika I
2. Naa Kalo (Naa Mahama), son of Naa Gbu-guma
3. Naa Toli (Naa Dahamani) son of Naa Abari-ka I
4. Naa Yakubu Savigu
5. Naa Wahu (Naa Abalsi)
6. Naa Ziblim Kuntibsa

7.  Naa Mahami

8.  Naa Haruna

9.  Naa Salifu, son of Naa Peinkpaa

10. Naa Abdulai Kurugu-kpaa 1926 – 1944

11. Naa Natogmah II, son of Dakpam-Naa At-
    tah 1944 – 1959

According to oral literature of some legends in Nanung, Naa Peinkpaa (Naa Natogmah I) was the one who beheaded Kpatihi Naa Napari somewhere in the 17th century and banned the Kpatihi Naa's title. Why was he killed? Because he interfered with Naa Peinkpaa when the Bimbilla skin title was due for him. Kpatihi Naa Napari was lobbying Bimbilla skin title for his uncle (Suburi Naa Nbang-zaa). Upon this, Kpatihi Naa Napari insulted Naa Peinkpaa when he was sitting on the Bimbilla Skin, an act which is an abomination in Nanung Chiefdom. These led to the conflict between Naa Peinkpaa and Kpatihi Naa Napari and Naa Peinkpaa beheaded him. From Naa Peinkpaa to Naa Natogmah Attah II, Warikpamo was the one who performed the enskinment rites. Naa Natogmah Attah II reactivated the Kpatihi Naa's title through Kpatihi Naa Yidaan-Togmah around 1944 – 1959. Why was it reactivated? There was a misunderstanding between Bomahi Naa Sheikakura and Yidaan-Togmah. Bomahi Naa Sheikakura insulted him that if he dies will he get a regent? Yidaan-Togmah could not contain the disgrace and quickly run to Naa Natogmah Attah II. Before the Kpatihi Naa's title was reactivated, Naa Natogmah observed a sacrifice for purification. In fact, Kpatihi Naa resumed his function on Naa Dassana Abdulai in 1959 to the late Naa Abarika Attah II in 1983 (just two Bimbilla chiefs). After Kpatihi-Naa Yidaan-Togmah, Kpatihi Naa Wumbei was next and followed by Kpatihi Naa Ponadow that is three Kpatihi Naas *(oral literature by Bimbilla Tolon Naa, Alhaji Braimah Damba, 2013)*. It is important to note that before the death of the late Naa Abarika Attah II, he, as president of the Nanumba Traditional Council, had summarily banned Kpatihi Naa from performing enskinment rites, according to the Bimbilla Lung-Naa Alhaji Abdulai. Since then, Warikpomo performs enskinment rites of all kinds of skin titles in Nanung. An example is Warikpomo Yahaya Abdulai performed the enskinment rites of DW2 (Wulehi Naa, Alhaji Salifu Wumbei) of this judgment during the period of Vo-Naa Attah Abarika was sitting on the Bimbilla skin as a Regent of Bimbilla Naa Abarika Attah II. Does it mean DW2 was not qualified as a kingmaker, yet he was invited by the Judicial Committee of the Northern Regional House of Chiefs? What adjective can one use to describe this? Was it also erroneous and faulty? The rhetorical question is: who appoints and performs the enskinment rites of Kpatihi Naa? Or he does it himself as the committee holds as facts? Conflict of interest to the highest degree! The custom and tradition of Nanung is unique. If one tries to play games with it, you would be caught just like the Judicial Committees of Northern Regional and National House Chiefs. Nanumbas have lived with this customary practice, norms, and tradition before the advent of German colony in the 18th century.

The judgment and declaration by the Judicial Committees

of the Northern Regional and National House of Chiefs that the 2nd defendant Azumah Natogmah is the acting regent of Kpatihi Naa, is a serious abomination according to the custom and tradition of Nanung where a direct younger brother of a late chief has been installed as a regent or acting regent. According to the custom and tradition of Nanung, situations where the chief who is late has no children or has only female children or the male children are underage. It allows for a nephew i.e., paternal line brother's son within the family to be installed as a regent and not direct younger brother. Even the Kpatihi Naa's title has no jurisdiction according to the custom of Nanung to install a sitting regent, because it is a subordinate title. It is a subordinate title because the kpatihi's title does not fall within divisional or subchiefs. Again, the rhetorical question is, under what authority by the custom of Nanung was he conferred this title of the so-called "acting regent of Kpatihi"? Or is it the committee that used its powers to confer on him this title?

The 2nd defendant is solidly behind the 1st defendant because the downfall of the first defendant means the 2nd defendant's family title "Kpatihi Naa" will not stand in Nanung or reactivated again.

The 1st and 2nd defendants are claiming from this judgment that the 1st petitioner is related to the Gbuguma-yili royal gate from maternal line is just a speculation rather than a fact. According to the custom of Nanung, female sons do not occupy Lepusi title because it is one of the gate system titles of the Gbuguma-yili as the rotational gate system is concern. If he is from the maternal line, why did his own father, Lepusi Naa Dawuni progress to Lepusi's title? Alternatively, are they trying to throw dust into the eyes of the public? Lepusi Naa Dawuni is the grandson of Naa Mahama Kalo, son of Naa Gbuguma. Why is he a grandson? Nabiyong (prince) Dahamani is the son of Naa Mahama Kalo, who married to a princess called Kasua, daughter of Nakpaa Naa Nyalignani (Nakpaa Naa Nahikurugu) and they gave birth to Lepusi Naa Dawuni. Naa Mahama Kalo and Nakpaa Naa Nyalignani were sons of Naa Gbuguma (Naa Azumah). It is clear from the above explanation that, Lepusi Naa Dawuni's maternal line is Nakpaa Naa Nyalignani family, and his paternal line is Naa Mahama Kalo's family. Nakpaa Naa Alhaji Salifu Dawuni or Naa Salifu Dawuni is the son of Lepusi Naa Dawuni who is 100% related to the Gbuguma-yili royal gate. His mother was known and called Balmini from Waribogu, a community from Dagbon. She was the first daughter of Waribogu-Lana Salifu. I wonder how somebody from Waribogu royal gate paternally could be related to the Gbuguma-yili royal gate of Nanung. Where is the maternal lineage of Nakpaa Naa Salifu Dawuni in the Gbuguma-yili Roya Gate? The Judicial Committees of Northern Region and National House of Chiefs hold the above claim by the 1st and 2nd defendants as a fact. From the explanations above clearly prove that Nakpaa Naa Salifu Dawuni has paternal lineage in the Gbuguma-yili Royal Gate of Nanung. With careful reading of the findings by the Judicial Committees of the Northern Region and National House Chiefs clearly shows that they were in bed with the 1st and 2nd defendants or politically influenced in their findings.

Moreover, the 1st defendant's grandfather, Naa Abdulai gave the Dakpam title to Dakpam Naa Dadinkai, who was also a great grandson from the Bang-yili royal gate. Why is he a great grandson? Dakpam Naa Bukali, regent of Naa Peinkpaa gave birth to Nabiyong (prince) Adam and Dakpam Naa Dadinkai is the son of Nabiyong (prince) Adam. It was because of his sudden death that denied him the Bimbilla skin title. The interesting question is that if great-grand sons are excluded, why was he given the Dakpam title? On the other hand, have they reviewed the custom of Nanung to exclude great-grand sons and closed the rotational gate system? If yes, when was the revision done and the composition of the team that reviewed it? This is where posterity awaits each and every one who play a role in setting things wrong in Nanung Kingdom under the guise of his or her office. One may run but cannot hide. The peace of Nanung is the peace of Northern Ghana; and the peace of Northern Ghana is the peace of the entire nation. This judgment is setting some precedence in Ghana and we lived to see its end. Still on the custom, when was the revision done to ignore the function of Juo Naa as the head of kingmakers who selects Bimbilla Naas and replaced with election where majority had to carry the vote? When and where was the election conducted on Bimbilla skin title and who supervised it? What was the composition of the Electoral College? The Bulsa Chiefdom of Sandema is the only Gbewaa chiefdom that apply election for the selection of Sandema Chief with well-defined electoral college. The electoral college comprises indigenous Bulsa Household Heads. The balloting is done opened. Meanwhile, other elections apply secret balloting. Hmmm, justice in Ghana favour's the highest bidder and not based on merit.

The 1st and 2nd petitioners and cross section of Nanumbas said the basis for the judgment in favour of the 1st and 2nd defendants was biased on the grounds that **the Judicial Committee of Northern Regional House of Chiefs contradicted itself in a previous judgement dated 3rd March 1993 and similarly chaired by YUNYOO-RANA YAMYIA TOOKA II which declared Nakpaa Naa Salifu (as he was then) as "eligible candidate for selection to the skin title of Nakpaa and that he like, any other great grandson of a Bimbilla Naa is not debarred by any known customary practice or usage from ascending the skin title of Bimbilla (Overload of Nanung) and for that matter the Nakpaa skin title of Bimbilla.".** Also, there is serious allegation of some high-profile politicians politically manipulated the verdict to score political points and amass votes, as it was an election year (2012 election). As a result, the 1st and 2nd petitioners filed an appeal on 16th March 2012 at the National House of Chiefs in Kumasi to seek justice. By the notice of appeal, the Appellants set down the following grounds of Appeal:

"1. The Judgment is against the weight of evidence.

2. Additional grounds to be filed upon re-

ceipt of the judgment

No additional grounds of appeal were filed until the 14$^{th}$ $^{of}$ August 2014.

The additional grounds of appeal are as follows:

1. That the judgment of the Judicial Committee of the Northern Regional House of Chiefs is a nullity.

2. The Judicial Committee of the Northern Regional House of Chiefs erred when it failed to appreciate that the customary law and usages relative to and pertaining to the enskinment of a Bimbilla Naa was peculiar to Nanung and not of a general application.

3. The Judicial Committee of the Northern Region House Chiefs erred when it held that the petitioners have no capacity to commence and maintain the action.

4. The Judicial Committee of the Northern Region House of Chiefs erred when it held that the 1$^{st}$ Petitioner/Appellant was ineligible to be enskinned as Bimbilla Naa.

5. The Judicial Committee of the Northern Region House of Chiefs

erred when it held that the enskinment of the 1st Respondent/Respondent as Bimbilla Naa was proper and in accordance with Nanung customary practice relative to the nomination and enskinment of Bimbilla Naa."

The findings of the Judicial Committee of the National House of Chiefs were not different from that of the Northern Regional House of Chiefs as discussed above. The Judicial Committee of the National House of Chiefs relied on the record of proceedings by the Judicial Committee of the Northern Region House of Chiefs. As such, the Judicial Committee of the National House of Chiefs dismissed the appeal and affirms the judgment of the Judicial Committee of the Northern Region House of Chiefs. However, I would like to discuss some of the most important record of proceedings they have quoted and cited in their judgment as bases of their decision to dismiss the appeal. These include the following:

1. The Judicial Committee of the National House of Chiefs erred when it held that the 2nd Appellant could not solely nominate a member of the Gbuguma-yili gate whose turn it is to ascend to the Bimbilla Skin title without involving the family. According to the Judicial Committee of the Nanumba Traditional Council that "Tradition catches and not majority carry the vote". Juo Naa is the head of kingmakers responsible for the selection of Bimbilla Naa. *For more information on*

*Juo Naa refer to chapter two (2) of this book with sub-title, Functions of Kingmakers.*

2. The Judicial Committee of the National House of Chiefs erred when it held that Juo Naa's selection of the Bakpaba Naa at the time was based on the fact that he was the head of the Bang-yili gate. According to rotational gate system titles of Nanung, Bakpaba Naa is not a title for Bang-yili. The Bakpaba Naa belongs to the Gbuguma-yili gate titles.

3. The Judicial Committee of the National House of Chiefs erred when it held that the DW2 Alhaji Salifu Wumbei, Wulensi Naa, said at page 498 of the record of appeal that: *"When Bimbilla Naa Natogmah died, there were two contestants, Nakpaa-Naa Dawuni and Bakpaba-Naa Dassana".* According to the history of Nanung, we have two Bimbilla Naas who were called Natogmah. Whether DW2 was referring to Bimbilla Naa Natogmah I (Naa Pienkpaa) or Bimbilla Naa Natogmah II (Naa Natogmah Attah)? Point of correction, there is no Bakpaba Naa Dassana in the history of Nanung. After the death of Bimbilla Naa Natogmah II there was a succession dispute between Bakpaba Naa Dawuni and Nakpaa Naa Dassana. *For more information refer to chapter three (3) of this book and also History of The Gbewaa Kingdoms Part I New Edition by Fusheini Yakubu, 2013 Chapter 4.*

4. The Judicial Committee of the National House of Chiefs erred when it held that Dakpam Naa Abukari from Bang-yili and Nakpaa Naa Attah from Gbuguma-yili were by passed because there were great grandsons. This is more of speculation rather than a fact. Dakpam Naa Abukari was the first son and regent of Bimbilla Naa Natogmah I (Naa Pienkpaa) from the Ban-yili gate. Bimbilla Naa Salifu I was the younger brother of Dakpam Naa Abukari. They were both sons of Bimbilla Naa Natogmah I. Why was Bimbilla Naa Salifu I being not by passed? How did he become a great grandson? Nakpaa Naa Attah is not also a great grandson. He was the son of Bimbilla Naa Shero and younger brother of Bakpaba Naa Iddrisa. Bakpaba Naa Iddrisa was the Regent of Bimbilla Shero. In the eyes of the law of the republic of Ghana, these are serious impersonations issue and for that matter an alleged criminal offence. Hmmm, that is justice in Ghana. Hence, justice in Ghana is for sale and for the highest bidder. Why should a credible Kingdom institution (National House of Chiefs) distort the history, custom and tradition of whole kingdom? Is it because of political, social, or economic influence? Bimbilla Naa Haruna was rather a grandson of Naa Azumah (Naa Gbuguma). Because Naa Gbuguma gave birth to Gundow Naa Gnunbaakum and he also gave birth to Bimbilla Naa Haruna. *For more information on Dakpam Naa Abukari and Nakpaa Naa Attah, refer to chapter three (3) of this book or History of the Gbewaa Kingdoms Part I New Edition by Fusheini Yakubu, 2013.*

5. The Judicial Committee of the National House of Chiefs erred when it held that from Gbuguma-yili gate, Naa Azumah from Jang who became Bimbilla Naa without passing through Nakpaa or Dakpam. According to the genealogy of Bimbilla Chiefs, there is only one Naa Azumah (Naa Gbuguma) who started the Gbuguma-yili gate when the rotational gate system in Nanung began. Naa Azumah used Nakpaa Naa's title to start the Gbuguma-yili, followed by Naa Nyong (Naa Imoro) from Dakpam, Bang-yili gate *(Genealogy of Nanung/Bimbilla Chiefs, History of the Gbewaa Kingdoms Part I New Edition Page 104 by Fusheini Yakubu, 2013). For more information refer to chapter three (3) of this book.* According to the gate system titles of both Gbuguma-yili and Bang-yili, there is no community or title called **Jang** as the Judicial Committee of the National House of Chiefs holds on page 11 of their judgment document.

6. Another interesting finding the Judicial Committee of the National House of Chiefs relied on is that *"some Bimbilla Naas who were not titles holders before they were enskinned were:*

   ❖ *Naa Sulgme, Naa Gmantambu's nephew who succeeded Naa Gmantambu. The title given to him before he was enskinned Bimbilla Naa was Bouling-Lana.*

   ❖ *Bimbilla Naa Dogiporigu. He was given the title*

*Pampapuia Naa before he ascended the skin"* and others.


It is interesting to note that those Bimbilla chiefs who were not title holders were conferred some titles before they were enskinned. Others used lesser titles of the rotational gate system to succeed Bimbilla Skin title. Which rotational gate system title did 1st Defendant used and who conferred the title on him? It was one Azumah (2nd Defendant) Natogmah who conferred on him a 'Kampakuya Naa'. According to the custom and tradition of Nanung, prince like the 1st Defendant is supposed to take a title from Bimbilla Naa, those with senior-most titles of the rotational gate system titles from their respective gates or the head of the council of elders (Kpihibara Naa). An example, the late Kpihibara Naa was the one who conferred Vogu title on the Regent of the late Bimbilla Naa Abarika Attah II before he was installed as a regent of Bimbilla Naa. Hence the so called Kampakuya Naa they claimed was conferred on the 1st Defendant was erroneous as far as the custom and tradition of Nanung is concern.


I wonder if the Judicial Committee of the Northern Region House of Chiefs recorded or used the actual proceedings of the Bimbilla chieftaincy case for the judgment. In order to validate this judgment, reference should be made to the proceedings of the Bimbilla chieftaincy case compiled by the Judicial Committee of the Northern Regional House of Chiefs.

The 1st and 2nd petitioners again, appealed the case at the Supreme Court of Ghana to further seek justice in 2018. On the 23rd of May 2018, the Supreme Court of Ghana dismissed the appeal by the 1st and 2nd petitioners and affirmed the decision of the National House Chiefs.

## 4.1 Contrariety of the Supreme Court Decision with Customary Laws and Practices of Nanumbas.

In its verdict, the Supreme Court made decisions in respect of the valid processes for ascending the Bimbilla skin title and the eligibility or qualification required to ascend the Bimbilla skin title.

These **decisions unfortunately do not accord with the customary practices of Nanumbas** and are viewed as impositions, the enforcement of which will disorganize the well-structured and properly regulated Chieftaincy institution in the Nanung Kingdom. Majority of Nanumbas are agitated by these "impositions" and have vowed to resist their application/enforcement. There is therefore a very high likelihood of violent conflict erupting anytime a new Bimbilla Naa is to be enskinned.

Highlights of these decisions and a discussion of their contrariety with customary laws and practices of Nanumbas are as follows:

4.2 Valid Processes for Ascending the Bimbilla Skin Title.

### 4.2.1 Nomination.

**Supreme Court Decision:** The family whose turn it is to occupy the Bimbilla Skin Title nominates a candidate for selection and enskinment by the Kingmakers.

**Nanung Custom and Practice:** This decision made by the supreme court does not accord with Nanung custom and practice. When the Bimbilla Skin falls vacant, a candidate who is interested in occupying the Skin communicates his interest directly to the Juo Naa or any of the other Kingmakers for the attention of the Juo Naa. (Minutes of Kingmakers 1983). The prospective candidate does not have to be nominated by his family before he expresses his interest. This should not be mistaken to mean that ascension of the Bimbilla Skin Title is open for all contests.

The quotations from the learned Justice S.A Brobbey in a passage at page 10 of his book titled **THE LAW OF CHEFTAINCY IN GHANA** and some case law might have influenced the Learned Judges to arrive at this decision which **unfortunately** is not applicable in Nanung. The Judicial Committee of the Northern Regional House Chiefs should have known this and refrained from giving this erroneous judgment which eventually was affirmed by the Supreme Court. The relevant passage reads:

*"Where there are two or more gates' families or houses from which to consider the next chief, and there is an established rotation system in the installation, the elders of the gate, family or house whose turn it is to appoint a chief will meet to consider the next person. They will nominate*

*and put forward the name of the next chief from the gate or house. The name of the selected candidate will then be submitted to the kingmakers who will consider his suitability."*

Page 146 paragraph 3 of the same book the learned author wrote:

*"Whoever makes the nomination has to do so in consultation with the appropriate members of the royal family or families entitled to nominate a candidate when their turn comes. In the case of In Re Kwabeng stool (supra) the Supreme Court held that failure to consult one of the three royal families rendered the nomination, election, and installation of the queen mother invalid for being contrary to custom. * Also, in the case of Republic vs.. Boateng, Ex party Adu-Gyamfi II [[1972] IGLR 317 in holding 7 thereof where the court held that where a party was not nominated by the queen mother or the royal family, his election and installation as a chief were irregular and contrary to custom".*

In other worlds a faulty nomination would affect the validity of election or installation or enskinment as in the instant appeal. The above decision from both the Northern Regional House of Chiefs and the National House of Chiefs affirmed by the Supreme Court of Ghana does not apply in Nanung which has its peculiar custom where the prospective candidates nominate themselves and allow the independent Council of Kingmakers to do a selection from among the self-nominated candidates.

As indicated under section above, the chieftaincy institution in Nanung Kingdom is well structured with skin titles hierarchically ranked to ensure discipline. Seniority of skin titles is respected and allows for a progression from the lesser Skins to the ultimate (Bimbilla skin title). The first three senior skin titles in ascending order are Gbungbalga Lana, Chamba Naa, and Dakpam Naa for the Bang-yili Royal gate and Jua Naa, Bakpaba Naa and Nakpaa Naa for the Gbugmayili royal gate. Contest for the Bimbilla skin is restricted to holders of these skin titles who spare no time in communicating their interest to the Juo Naa and other Kingmakers without recourse to their families. Thus, nomination of a candidate by his family is not a requirement for his enskinment and neither will his enskinment be a nullity simply because his family did not nominate him.

This must not be confused with the role of the Bimbilla Naa in enskinning sub-chiefs. The Bimbilla Naa may consult with families of persons he intends to enskin as sub-chiefs before selecting them.

## 4.2.2 Selection

**Supreme Court Decision:** Juo Naa is not everything in the selection process of a Bimbilla Naa. The other kingmakers have a say as to who is finally selected.

**Nanung Custom and Practice:** Upon receipt of the expression of interest for the Bimbilla Skin Title, the Juo Naa consults the Deities/Gods and ancestors of the land through soothsaying for a revelation of the most suitable candidate to be made to him. He then selects that candidate and informs the other king makers about his choice. The other kingmakers consider and endorse his choice. In the unlikely event that the Juo Naa's choice is not endorsed, he will go into seclusion from where he will consult the deities again and come back to his colleague Kingmakers with the choice of candidate revealed to him. No other Kingmaker is vested with the power and authority to select the candidate. Since the evolution of the two-gate rotational system, the selection of a candidate occupy the Bimbilla Skin Title has been on Dakpam for Bang-yili and Nakpaa for Gbuguma-yili as the latest transition. Nanumba Kingdom has lived with this customary practice for more than two centuries.

The other Kingmakers then assist the Juo Naa in various roles to perform other customary rites on the selected candidate to signify the latter's enskinment. These customary rites include:

- Presenting cola nuts to the selected candidate.
- Escorting the selected candidate to the palace of the deceased Bimbilla Naa to meet the Juo Naa.
- Cleansing or bathing the selected candidate with special herbal bath prepared by the Juo Naa and finally,
- Enrobing the selected candidate.

### 4.2.3 Enskinment

**Supreme Court decision:** The Kpatihi Na has custody of Bimbilla Naa's regalia and he enskins Bimbilla Naa.

**Nanung Custom and Practice:** The Kpatihi Naa does not enskin the Bimbilla Naa but instead he enrobes the candidate selected to-be Bimbilla Naa on the express instruction of the Juo Naa. Kpatihi Naa cannot perform that function unless he is directed by the Juo Naa to do so. The Juo Naa may also delegate any other kingmaker to enrobe the Bimbilla Naa.

In fact, in the judgement of the Judicial Committee of the Northern Regional House of Chiefs chaired by YUNYOO-RANA YAMYIA TOOKA II in a chieftaincy dispute in 1993 over the enskinment of Nakpaa Naa, chairman described Kpatihi Naa's role in enskinning a chief as a delegated function and not the prerogative of the Kpatihi Naa. Any of the Kingmakers can therefore be instructed by the Juo Naa to play that role in the enskinment process and that enskinment will be valid.

In Nanung custom, enskinment of a Bimbilla Naa entails selecting a candidate, presenting the candidate with cola nuts, cleansing, or bathing the candidate with special herbal water and enrobing the candidate. Thus, as part of the process of enskinning a Bimbilla Naa the selected candidate is enrobed with a sacred regalia which was used to enrobe the founder of the Nanung kingdom, Naa Gmantambu and other past Bimbilla chiefs. This regalia is jealously protected by kingmakers of Nanung and is currently in the custody of Kpatihi Naa to be used as and when the need arises and on the instruction of Juo Naa.

The validity of enskinment of a Bimbilla Naa is not dependent on the personality or official who has enrobed him but rather it is dependent on the authorization of the Juo Naa, who is the chairman of the Kingmakers.

## 4.3 Eligibility and Qualification of a Candidate to be Enskinned Bimbilla Naa.

### 4.3.1 Ascension of the Nakpaa Naa and Dakpam Naa to the Bimbilla skin automatic.

**Supreme Court Decision:** Whereas an incumbent Nakpaa Naa or Dakpam Naa, depending on whose Gate's turn it is to occupy a vacant Bimbilla skin title has a high probability of being made the Bimbilla Naa; he does not have an automatic right to the skin. Where there are circumstances considered justifiable the kingmakers may bypass an incumbent Nakpaa Naa or Dakpam Naa upon the scrutiny by Juo Naa as the case may be.

**Nanung Custom and Practice:** As indicated earlier the skin titles in Nanung are hierarchically ranked. The Nakpaa Naa is the highest ranked skin title for the Gbuguma-yili Gate whiles the Dakpam Naa is the highest ranked skin title for the Bang-yili Gate. The incumbents of these two apices ranked skin titles take turns to ascend the vacant Bimbilla skin. It is only when there are no incumbents to these two skins or when the incumbents have not expressed interest to contest for the Bimbilla skin title that the kingmakers consider incumbents of other lower ranked Skins in order of seniority for enskinment.

As explained in section above this rotation between Nakpaa Naa and Dakpam Naa for the ascension of the Bimbilla skin title was established right after theevolution of the Two-gate system.

Since the evolution of the rotational gate system, eighteen (18) chiefs ascended to the Bimbilla Skin. Out of the eighteen (18) Bimbilla Chiefs enskinned so far, fourteen (14) of them have either been incumbent Nakpaa Naa or Dakpam Naa. Only four of them used other titles with peculiar situations.

## 4.3.2 Eligibility of Great Grandsons to Ascend the Bimbilla Skin Title

**Supreme Court Decision:** Great grandsons of a Bimbilla Naa do not qualify to ascend the Bimbilla skin title. Only paternal sons and grandsons qualify.

**Nanung Custom and Practice:** Contest for the Bimbilla skin title is restricted to incumbents of the first three ranked skins of Jua, Bakpaba and Nakpaa for the Gbuguma-yili Gate and Gbungbalga, Chamba and Dakpam for the Bang-yili Gate. Incumbents of these skins are eligible or are qualified to ascend the Bimbilla skin irrespective of their status as SONS, GRANDSONS OR GREAT GRANDSONS. They must however have patrilineal linage to the Bimbilla Skin Title.

It is important to reiterate that under the customary law of Ghana, those who are deemed qualified to become chiefs are those who belong to the Royal Clan. In this regard, under customary law in Ghana, there are two types of family relationships in Ghana: maternal and paternal. The common thread in all these systems is whether one can trace his ancestry to a common ancestor, paternally or maternally depending on the family system one belongs. In Re ADUM Stool, Agyei v for [1998-1999] SCGLR191, "it was held as follows: (1) A person's immediate family in a patrilineal community would consist of his children, either male or female, his paternal brothers and sisters, paternal grandfather and descendants of the paternal uncles in the direct male lines. His wider family would consist of the immediate families of all those who trace their ancestry through the common male ancestor".

1. Furthermore, in the classic work on Customary Law in Ghana **--THE LAW OF INTEKINGDOM AND TEKINGDOM SUCCESSION IN GHANA, N.A. OLLENU at page 171 Kingdoms:** *"In the patrilineal system, the family which succeeds is the group traced from a male ancestor in the direct male line".* It is against these propositions under the customary law of Ghana, that the attempt to limit only those qualified to succeed to sons and grandsons and to the exclusion of great grandsons, is self-seeking and not supported by law, because the emphasis is on whether a person can trace his lineage to a common male ancestor. In Nanung there is nowhere in our history where this bizarre imposition has ever been agreed upon by the stakeholders within the chieftaincy clans, either verbally or written. (The Ugly Legacy of an Over-Ambitious Prince of Nanung (Fusheini Yakubu, 11th February 2018).

It is important to note that, The Judicial Committee of the Northern Regional House of Chiefs that sat on the Nakpaa issue in 1993 was chaired by the **YUNYOO-RANA YAMYIA TOOKA II.** He was supported on the Committee by the Sunsong Naa Shani Hamid and Yelzoli-Lana Salifu Dramani. The Committee after several sittings came out with their verdict as follows:

- That the committee was unable to grant the reliefs the petitioners were seeking on account of the following amongst others:

- The claim that great grandchildren were debarred from ascending the Nakpaa Skin Title was dismissed.

Indeed, in the concluding remarks of the Committee on the issue of his disqualification on account of he being a great grandson, the Committee had this to say: "Under the circumstances, the Committee holds that 2nd Defendant (NAA Salifu Dawuni) was an eligible candidate for selection to the Skin Title of Nakpaa and that he, like any other great grandson of a Bimbilla Naa IS NOT DEBARRED by any known customary practice or usage from ascending the Ultimate Skin Title of Bimbilla and for that matter the Nakpaa Skin Title of Bimbilla". (EXHIBIT 1983: Minutes of Kingmakers meeting in the selection of a candidate for the Bimbilla Skin Title).

Following the outcome of the verdict passed by the Judicial Committee, the Petitioners filed an Appeal at the National House of Chiefs. The case was, however, struck out for want of prosecution when the petitioners on several occasions failed to show up when the case was called by the Judicial committee of the National House of Chiefs and a fine imposed on them. (EXHIBIT 1993 Ruling of the Judicial Committee of the National House of Chiefs on the Nakpaa case).

### 4.3.4 Eligibility of Non-Titled Princes to Ascend the Bimbilla Skin Title.

**Supreme Court Decision:** It is permissible to confer the chieftainship title Kankapuya Naa on a Prince in order for him to ascend the Bimbilla Skin Title.

**Nanung Custom and Practice:** Certain titles including Kankapuya Naa, Bolin Lana, Vo-Naa, etc. have no Skins attached to them. They are honorary titles conferred ONLY on Regents of Bimbilla "Nanima"/ chiefs to enable them act as Bimbilla Naa until their fathers' funerals are performed. With the adoption of the rotational gate system in Nanung, a Regent of a Bimbilla Naa **CAN NOT** ascend the Bimbilla skin after he has performed his father's funeral but has to pass on the skin title to the next Bimbilla Naa from the other gate. He is then given a lesser skin to enable him to learn to govern and progress to the Bimbilla skin title.

Thus, these HONORARY titles are not conferred on just any ordinary Bimbilla Prince but on REGENTS only. And they are conferred not to enable them to ascend the Bimbilla skin title but to enable them to take their late fathers' stead and ACT as Bimbilla Naa.

It is not in doubt that there have been occasions in the past where non-title holders adopted and used previously non-existing titles in the Nanumba traditional area. Naa Sulgme adopted the title Bolin from Dagbon because in the first place this was in the formative years or the conquer and rule era of the chieftaincy institutions among the people of Nanung and secondly the rotating system of the chieftaincy in Nanung had not been established. That apart Naa Sulgme was the chosen heir of Naa Gmantambu, the Founder of Nanung Kingdom and for that matter a Regent who could be given an honorary title to act as Bimbilla as explained above and later enskinned. Indeed, this is an isolated case and cannot be used to justify a finding in favour of Mr. Andani Dassana enskinment as Bimbilla Naa. It is important to note that the chieftaincy institution of Nanung like any other sister Gbewaa Kingdoms has gone through a number of transitions such as traditional catching of chiefs to their current customary practices and usages. As such, the current transition of Nanung Custom and Usage is the Two Gate Rotational System (Nakpaa for Gbuguma-yili and Dakpam Bang-yili).

The other chief mentioned as having been enskinned Bimbilla Naa without a lesser skin title is Naa Salifu Nantogmah. His example is erroneous because he was a Bimbilla Naa who the colonial administrators, the Germans detained and later released. A caretaker Bimbilla Naa was appointed in his absence. After the caretaker Bimbilla Naa died, he was selected to retake the Bimbilla Skin Title. Naa Salifu Nantogmah cannot therefore also be cited as somebody who did not have a skin title before being enskinned Bimbilla Naa for the second time. According to Bang-yili submission to the Sole Mediator, His Royal Highness Togbi Sri III is that "although it is true that Naa Sulgme adopted a previously non-title among Nanumbas, this is isolated and cannot justify a finding in favour to the enskinment of Mr. Andani Dassana. Naa Dogi-Poriga (same)". Naa Salifu Nantogmah was arrested by the Germans who took him to Kete Krachi. On his return he had no title but was re-inKingdomd when a vacancy occurred, and it was the turn of Bang-yili Gate to present a candidate (Bimbilla Naa). This is also an isolated case and there is no deskinment in Nanung. No Nanumba chief can be deskinned. The elders concluded that the chief was not dead and no ritual funeral "Nakuli" had been performed which is the only condition for succession the customary alternation between the two royal gates was not permissible (SUPRA Exhibit 7).

# CHAPTER 5

## THE IMPACT OF BIMBILLA CHIEFTAINCY CONFLICT.

### 5.0 Introduction.

The writer considers this chapter as a very relevant area for discussion to educate readers on the effects of the chieftaincy conflict that has bedeviled Nanung for more than two decades. Gone are the days, when succession disputes to the Bimbilla skin title were resolved with less time spent, even before the advent of the Whiteman (Colonial Masters). I wonder in this Millennium and the 21st Century, with the computerized system, well established legal institutions and structures coupled with high-level legal luminaries that were unable to resolve chieftaincy succession case sustainably because justice is always compromised for jury as a result of political, social, or economic interest. Even when we spent more than a decade in an attempt to resolve a case, it does not yield results and resources are wasted. Why is it so? Is it because of fear or favour for any of the party's (petitioners or defendants)? Is it corruption that has weakened our justice system, structures, and morality? We claim that this is the era of globalization, yet we are unable to resolve similar issues our great grandfathers used less time and resources to resolve them sustainably.

It is rather unfortunate; with the advent of technology, we are still lacking behind in this direction. Time has come for us to revisit certain values our great grandfathers cherished in the past to improve our morality and integrity.

## 5.1 Socio-Cultural Effects.

### 5.1.1 Destabilization of the Structure of the Council of Kingmakers.

At all material times, the Juo Naa has been recognized as the Head or Chairman of the Council of Kingmakers. Indeed, he is the primus inter-pares among his colleagues.

Since the founding of the Nanung Kingdom this revered chief has played a key role in the enskinment of Bimbilla chiefs "Nanima". The same cannot be said of the Kpatihi Naa whose office / title at some time in the history of the Nanung never existed. He was co-opted to the Council of Kingmakers as late as 1958 and only performs functions that are delegated to him by the Bimbilla Naa or the Juo Naa. The Supreme Court verdict has however overrated him to such an extent that his office is superior to that of the Juo Naa and even the Bimbilla Naa in that, one becomes a Bimbilla Naa at his pleasure. Also, the verdict empowers him to defy instructions given to him by the Head of the Kingmakers, the Juo Naa.

### 5.1.2 Shorn of Indiscipline by Princes.

The age-old tradition which ensured Royals were installed chiefs in a promotional system that is, they became chiefs of smaller settlements and moved to higher chieftaincy positions until if eligible, they aspired to the Kingship position of Bimbilla Naa has been jettisoned and a "new tradition" that lacks clarity and a clearly defined path for ascending the Bimbilla skin imposed on the Nanumbas.

### 5.1.3 Indiscriminate enskinment of Chiefs.

Under Nanung custom and usage, a Regent of a Bimbilla Naa is prohibited from enskinning chiefs to Dakpam, Nakpaa, Chamba, Bakpaba, Gbungbalga and Jua Traditional areas as these skins are highly ranked and serve as gate skins titles whose incumbents can contest and be selected and enskinned as Bimbilla Naa. Regrettably however, a Regent of one of the Disputants has enskinned chiefs to four (4) of these skins in flagrant disregard of this century old Nanung custom.

### 5.2 Socio-Economic Effects.

Most businesspersons in Nanung during this feud are beset with certain limitations to access big credit facilities from big financial institutions such as banks because there is no substantive chief to endorse their land documents for an indenture that will qualify them to access bigger loan facilities from the banks. Secondly, where there is conflict, corruption is also at its peak simply because there is no unity among the people. As such, public officers take advantage of the situation for exploitation at the expense of development. Funds that are meant for development are always spent on security. The security takes advantage of this situation to harass residents in their homes under cover of curfew. In view of this, residents find it difficult to even make phone-calls during curfew hours. People who fall sick at night cannot be taken to hospital and this increases number of deaths. Businesses that were to be transacted early in the morning had to start late and one can imagine the impact it will have on society.

## 5.3 Effects on Politics.

Politicians always take advantage of chieftaincy conflicts in one way or the other to attract votes. This situation is relative with critical examination. They are sometimes successful in some cases. On the other hand, it turns against them (*study election patterns for 2000, 2004, 2008, 2012, 2016, and 2020*). When such situations occur, democracy begins to limp. It does not provide an enabling environment for democracy or partisan politics to strive within a given period. Competent candidates are sometimes denied the opportunity to serve their people and the nation at large just because he/she has been identified with a particular chieftaincy faction. This practice by politicians is very dangerous to their success. The situation should rather be handled by Governments and politicians with caution and care as it punctures the peace of a nation. For democracy to be effective devoid of chieftaincy and ethnic influence, both governments and politicians should take interest in resolving chieftaincy and ethnic conflicts in fairness and for peace and stability. Mediation has been more successful than the court settlement in the context of chieftaincy. Traditional Rulers complement the efforts of governments for growth and development in their respective areas and the nation at large.

## 5.4 Proposals for Amicable Resolution Of The Dispute.

After carefully examination of events in the dispute and mindful of the tension and uneasy calm currently prevailing in the Nanung Kingdom, I therefore, wish to propose the following for the consideration of the Sole Mediator, His Royal Highness Togbi Sri III as he seeks an amicable resolution of the Bimbilla Chieftaincy dispute:

A. The Sole mediator could facilitate the resolution of the intra gate feud within the Gbuguma-yili Royal gate by giving them a roadmap to perform the funerals of the two Disputants who are both deceased. This will pave the way for the enskinment of a new Bimbilla Naa from the Bang-yili gate as a matter of urgency.

B. Nakpaa Naa Salifu Dawuni was enskinned Bimbilla Naa in accordance with the customs and traditions of Nanumbas and ought to be recognized as such. It is also worth noting that majority of Nanumbas recognized him as the legitimate overlord i.e., Bimbilla Naa. He should therefore be given a befitting funeral as a Bimbilla Naa before the enskinment of a new Bimbilla Naa. This gesture will assure Nanumbas that they can continue to practice their cherished customs in so far as the enskinment of a Bimbilla Naa is concerned.

C. The "Gate Skin Title" concept where Nakpaa skin Title and Dakpam Skin Title become the conduit for ascending to the Bimbilla Skin Title should be maintained. In the event that there are no incumbents on these skin Titles' occupants of lesser skin titles in the hierarchy of the gate skin titles can be considered.

D. The authority of the Juo Naa should be restored by the Sole Mediator assisting the Kingmakers to understand their rightful duties and spelling these out for them.

E. The enskinment of chiefs of whatever type should be frozen until a new Bimbilla Naa is enskinned.

F. Chiefs who have been given titles indiscriminately should be reviewed.

G. The committee should ensure that a hierarchical succession to the Bimbilla Skin Title should not be limited to sons and grandsons of Bimbilla Naa's.

H. Steps should be taken to document succession in Nanung Kingdom.

I. Any new custom that is to be introduced into Nanung of any novelty into Nanung Chieftaincy, it MUST not be unilateral but must be discussed at the traditional Council for inputs by all relevant stakeholders from all the diverse Chieftaincy divides (BANG-YILI AND GBUGMA-YILI) for possible approval or rejection.

# APPENDIX I: GENEALOGY OF NANUNG/BIMBILLA CHIEFS

1 Naa Gmantambu, son of Naa Gbewaa
2 Naa Sulgme
3 Naa Kumkayoɣri, son of Gmantambu
4 Naa Dogiporigu, son of Sulgme
5 Naa Badariga
6 Naa Naɣi Baarigu
7 Naa Saa
8 Naa Koŋa
9 Naa Kunbalinkulga
10 Naa Nyelinbolgu, son of Kunbalinkulga
11 Naa Wobgu (Naa Pampamli or Mahamuda)
12 Naa Saa-kpang (Naa Damba) son of Nyelinbolgu
13 Naa Sulgu (Naa Maamani), son of Wobgu/Mahamuda
14 Naa Gbuguma (Naa Azuma), son of Nakpaa Naa Sanboni
15 Naa Nyong (Naa Imoro), son of Naa Damba
16 Naa Bulali-bila (Naa Kurugu-kpaa) son of Nakpaa-Naa Sanboni
17 Naa Abarika I, (Naa Bang) son of Dakpam-Naa Kpanjogu
18 Naa Shero, son of Naa Gbuguma
19 Naa Natogmah I (Naa Peinkpaa), son of Naa Abarika I
20 Naa Kalo (Naa Mahama), son of Naa Gbuguma
21 Naa Toli (Naa Dahamani) son of Naa Abarika I
22 Naa Yakubu Savigu
23 Naa Wahu (Abalsi)

24  Naa Ziblim Kuntibsa

25  Naa Mahami

26  Naa Haruna son of Gundow Naa Gnunbaakum

27  Naa Salifu, son of Naa Peinkpaa

28  Naa Abdulai Kurugu-kpaa 1926 – 1944

29  Naa Natogmah II, son of Dakpam-Naa Attah 1944 – 1959

30  Naa Dassana, son of Naa Abdulai 1959 – 1981

31  Naa Abarika Attah II, son of Dakpam-Naa Attah 1983 – 1999

# BIBLOGRAPHY

An Ethnographic study of Northern Ghana's conflicts towards sustainable peace by A.K Awoedoba:2009.

Bang-yili Royal Gate Position Paper Submission to the Sole Mediator, His Royal Highness Togbi Sri III on Bimbilla Chieftaincy Dispute, January 2020.

Bimbilla Lung-Naa, oral Literature source, 2008.

CV of Nakpaa-Naa Alhaji Salifu Dawuni.

Chieftaincy Succession Dispute in Nanung, Northern Ghana: Interrogating the Narratives of the Contestants (By Alhassan Sulemana Anamzoya & Steve Tonah).

Chieftaincy Matters-Areas of Research Northern Region.

Chiefdom at War with Chief less People while the Kingdom Look On (By Peter **Skalník,** University of Hradec Králové).

Fusheini Yakubu, History of the Gbewaa Kingdoms – Part I, New Edition, 2013.

Ibrahim Mahama    - History and Tradition of Dagbon, 2004.


Law of Chieftaincy in Ghana: S.A. Brobby.


Minutes of Kingmakers Meeting in the Selection of a Candidate for the Bimbilla Paramountcy Held on Monday 31st January 1983.


Nanumba District Profile, 1996.


Nanumba District Economic Development Plan, 1996.


Political Anthropology Vol. 7-outwitting Ghana: Pluralism of Political culture in Nanung by Peter Skalnik page 149 paragraph 2) 1992


Shinnie, P. and P. Ozanne, 1972 excavation at Yani Dabari, Transaction of the Historical Society of Ghana No. 6.


The Judicial Committee of Nanumba Traditional council, "Gumah Commission report", 2003.

The Judicial Committee of the Northern Region House of Chiefs Judgment of the Bimbilla chieftaincy case on 13th March 2012.

The Chieftaincy Tribunal of the National House of Chiefs Apeal Court, Kumasi sitting on Wednesday 22nd November 1995.

The Chieftaincy Tribunal of the National House of Chiefs Appeal Court, Kumasi sitting on Thursday 12th February 1998.

The Judicial Committee of the National House of Chiefs Judgment of the Bimbilla chieftaincy case on 8th October 2014.

The Supreme Court of Ghana Judgment on Bimbilla Chieftaincy Case on 23rd of May 2018.

The tribes of the Ashanti Hinterland Vol 2: Oxford Clarendon Press; Rattray R.S (1932).

The Ugly Legacy of an Over-Ambitious Prince of Nanung (Fusheini Yakubu, 11th February 2018).

www.ingramcontent.com/pod-product-compliance
Lightning Source LLC
Chambersburg PA
CBHW060249030426
42335CB00014B/1635